British History in Perspective
General Editor: Jeremy Black

PUBLISHED TITLES

D1344938

Please note that a sister series, *Social History in Perspective*, is now available. It covers the key topics in social, cultural and religious history.

British History in Perspective
Series Standing Order
ISBN 0–333–71356–7 hardcover
ISBN 0–333–69331–0 paperback
(*outside North America only*)

You can receive future titles in this series as they are published by placing a standing order. Please contact your bookseller or, in case of difficulty, write to us at the address below with your name and address, the title of the series and one or both of the ISBNs quoted above.

Customer Services Department, Macmillan Distribution Ltd
Houndmills, Basingstoke, Hampshire RG21 6XS, England

VICTORIAN POLITICAL THOUGHT

H. S. JONES

First published in Great Britain 2000 by
MACMILLAN PRESS LTD
Houndmills, Basingstoke, Hampshire RG21 6XS and London
Companies and representatives throughout the world

A catalogue record for this book is available from the British Library.

ISBN 0–333–56537–1 hardcover
ISBN 0–333–56538–X paperback

First published in the United States of America 2000 by
ST. MARTIN'S PRESS, INC.,
Scholarly and Reference Division,
175 Fifth Avenue, New York, N.Y. 10010

ISBN 0–312–22902–X

Library of Congress Cataloging-in-Publication Data
Jones, H. S. (H. Stuart)
Victorian political thought / H.S. Jones.
    p.   cm. — (British history in perspective)
Includes bibliographical references and index.
ISBN 0–312–22902–X (cloth)
1. Political science—Great Britain—History—19th century.
I. Title.   II. Series.
JA84.G7J65   1999
320.941'09'034—dc21   99–41293
                                                            CIP

This book is printed on paper suitable for recycling and made from fully managed and
sustained forest sources.

10   9   8   7   6   5   4   3   2   1
09 08 07 06 05 04 03 02 01 00

Printed in Hong Kong

For Hilary

CONTENTS

INTRODUCTION

In the past three decades the study of the history of political thought has undergone a remarkable renewal, accompanied by vigorous methodological debate about the proper way of studying past political thought. But in the course of this renewal the most exciting work has dealt with the early modern period, and some of the distinctive problems in writing the history of late modern political thought have been overlooked. More than most historians of political thought, those who write about the nineteenth and twentieth centuries tend to be tugged in two opposite directions: on the one hand towards high theory, on the other towards the doctrines propounded by and on behalf of organized political movements. It is only when we reach the age of ideologies that it becomes possible to cast the history of political thought as a history of *isms* in which the leading thinkers appear in the guise of representatives of one doctrine or another.

This is not the place to engage in an extended dissertation on the merits of different approaches to the history of political thought. But it is right to make it clear at the outset what sort of book this is. I have not set out to write a history of ideologies. The reader will find a good deal here about liberalism and conservatism, about nationalism, radicalism and socialism; but these are not the categories around which the book is constructed. It is a book about thought and about thinkers. My starting point is the postulate that what characterizes political thinkers – what marks them off from others who argue a political cause in terms of abstract values such as 'liberty' or 'democracy' or 'tradition' or 'community' – is a deeper and reflective concern with the sources of political value: what *counts* as a valid argument in politics? In their different ways the two Mills and Macaulay, Carlyle and Arnold, Spencer and Bagehot, Green and Bosanquet, Kidd and the Webbs were concerned with that sort of question. So too, perhaps, was Gladstone. Most Victorian statesmen, and most other activists, were not. That is my justification for giving certain texts a degree of priority over the shapeless mass of Victorian political discourse.

ix

At the same time historians of political thought have rightly come to
appreciate that the authors of 'great texts' were not engaged in a her-
metic conversation with each other. While Plato and Aristotle, Rousseau
and Hegel were, at various times, important presences in Victorian
political thought, the arguments of the political thinkers were not sealed
off from 'Victorian political discourse'. Bosanquet, for instance, could
vindicate a version of Rousseau's concept of the general will in a volume
of essays on the social problem published under the auspices of the
Charity Organization Society.[1] The thinkers under discussion were, in
varying degrees, political actors, and it would be naïve to suppose that
their practical stances were derived from their abstract positions. One of
the engines of conceptual change in political thought is political innovation: the need to defend new political realities or objectives, or old realities against new challenges. We cannot gain a proper understanding of
Arnold or Mill or Spencer without an appreciation of the assumptions
they shared with their contemporaries, and of the ways in which they
differed from them – how, for instance, they used familiar political
vocabularies for new and unexpected purposes.

To define a political thinker as one who reflects about what counts as
a valid argument in politics has peculiar force in a study of nineteenth-
century political thought. The leading thinkers studied in this book –
Arnoldians and Fabians, evolutionists and idealists, not to mention utilitarians as different as J. S. Mill and Henry Sidgwick – practically all felt
that they were living in a transitional age, the distinctive characteristic
of which was precisely its lack of agreement about political, social and
ethical values. The desperate need of the age was for a new intellectual
synthesis. Carlyle, lamenting the decay of 'the Metaphysical and Moral
Sciences' in an 'Age of Machinery', pleaded for their renewal so as to
institute a 'right coordination' of the mechanical and dynamical prov-
inces.[2] F. D. Maurice, who believed that a 'society founded upon opinions
had no real cohesion', declared in a discussion of Comtean positivism
that he too was engaged in a quest for 'the only possible doctrine for an
age of science', though his view of what that doctrine was differed from
Comte's.[3] In the mid-Victorian period the problem of political order
became less pressing as the spectre of revolution or anarchy receded.
But the problem of intellectual and moral authority was if anything
more pressing rather than less in the age of Darwinism and the Higher
Criticism; and the quest for political order was transmuted into the quest
for the laws of progress. 'Never, surely, was the English mind so confused, so wanting in fixed moral principles, as at present', complained

Sir John Seeley in an address to the Cambridge Ethical Society in 1888.
A few years later the social evolutionist Benjamin Kidd lamented 'the
almost complete absence of any clear indication from those who speak in
the name of science and authority as to the direction in which the path of
future progress lies. On every side in those departments of knowledge
which deal with social affairs change, transition, and uncertainty are
apparent.'[4] These thinkers agreed on the need for a new synthesis, but
they disagreed about who or what could provide the foundation for such
a synthesis. Would it be the political economists who, once they had with
Mill's help resolved the 'unsettled questions' of their discipline, would
set forth a coherent model for an authoritative 'moral science'? Or
would it be a revamped and modernized elite, a clerisy educated in the
reformed and truly 'national' public schools and universities and aiming
to reinfuse the state with a moral purpose by means of a truly national
and undogmatic church? Or would the natural sciences, which to many
critics bore the responsibility for the intellectual upheavals of the age,
themselves furnish the only workable form of authority in the modern
age? Would scientists become, as Francis Galton hoped, 'a sort of scientific priesthood', enjoying the cultural authority and social status once
vested in the Anglican clergy, and shaping public opinion in the light of
scientific knowledge.[5] Would it prove possible, as Leslie Stephen hoped,
to forge an evolutionary science of ethics on the model of evolutionary
biology, and possessed of comparable authority? These different ways of
addressing the problem of authority constitute the organizing principles
of this study.

The decision to organize the book around these three clusters of
potentially authoritative discourses is evidently a matter of personal
interpretation. Others will think that a different structure would have
distorted the content rather less. This study focuses on the intellectual
élites and has less to say about, for instance, the political culture of provincial nonconformity. But it should be borne in mind that from the
1860s the cultural and intellectual élite became much more cohesive, as
the ancient universities largely succeeded in regaining their 'national'
standing and intellectual ascendancy. Furthermore, I would argue that
my presentation helps us to understand British political thought in
European terms. For the basic problem that confronted Victorian thinkers, as I have stated it, was one that preoccupied continental thinkers
from the era of the French Revolution onwards, just as it preoccupied
their British counterparts. Hegel and Saint-Simon, Lamennais and
Comte, all pursued the aim of 'closing' what they perceived as an era of

spiritual anarchy devoid of intellectual authority and hence of social harmony. Their analysis of the distinctive problems of their age was echoed by John Stuart Mill, in his essays on 'Bentham', 'Coleridge', and 'The Spirit of the Age', as well as by thinkers as different as Coleridge himself, Carlyle and Dr Arnold. There were some peculiarities in the answers offered by British thinkers. Political economy, which in Britain for a time seemed within reach of the standing of an authoritative discipline, was always much more controversial on the continent, where (in France for instance) its claims were contested by republican left and Catholic right; so that Comte, unlike Mill, refused to base his science of society on the model of a classical political economy which rested on hedonistic psychological assumptions. And no continental nation, not even France, could rival English historians' self-confident identification of their national history with the growth of constitutional liberty. Nevertheless British political thought was not as insular as is often thought, and that is a point I hope to make clearer in the course of this study. To take just two examples for the time being: the idea of nationality was as important to Victorian thinkers as it was to their continental counterparts, and the greatest ideologue of nineteenth-century European democratic nationalism, Mazzini, was fêted by English progressive thinkers. He and Marx – perhaps the two most influential political thinkers in nineteenth-century Europe – both wrote a large part of their work in England. Secondly, the ethical preoccupations that accompanied the 'crisis of faith' in the last decades of the century were by no means as uniquely English as might be imagined: very similar concerns with the foundations of morality shaped the work of French social thinkers such as Fouillée and Durkheim.

Two peculiarities of nineteenth-century political thought merit brief discussion here, because they shape the ways in which a history of the subject can be written. This was the first age in which the character of political thought was shaped by a consciousness of its own history. It was the Victorians who invented the study of the history of political thought – often, in academic terms, under the heading of 'political science' – and a good number of the leading intellectuals of the period were themselves engaged in the study of the history of ideas. John Morley and Leslie Stephen were just the most notable examples. Furthermore, the writers who, after Stephen, pioneered the study of Victorian political thought – such men as Ernest Barker, A. D. Lindsay and Harold Laski – were themselves products of late-Victorian currents of thought such as idealism and pluralism, and in their histories were engaged in a sort of intellectual dialogue with the traditions they took as their subjects. Thus Barker's book begins by defining its subject in classically idealist terms: 'Political philosophy in itself, and apart from other studies, is essentially an ethical study, which regards the State as a moral society, and inquires into the ways by which it seeks to attain its ultimate moral aim.' It ends with an endorsement of one of the central claims of pluralism, the need for 'a new conception of the State, and more especially a new conception of sovereignty'.[6] So the early historiography was closely bound up with the subject itself. It would be illuminating to have a full-scale study of the historiography of Victorian political thought which took up this line of inquiry.

Furthermore, the study of the history of ideas – whether the history of political thought or the still more fashionable study of the history of ethics – was itself an integral component of the quest for authority which I have sketched above. William Thomas has suggested that one of the reasons why the utilitarians came to be seen as exercising a domin-ant influence over the political outlook of the early and mid-Victorian period was that many late-Victorian liberals, viewing the philosophic radicals through the prism of J. S. Mill's *Autobiography* – itself rather an exercise in the history of ideas than a straightforward account of his life – came to exaggerate and envy the certainty and unity which they thought they found in that school, and which they longed for in their own age. The Liberal politician and historian John Morley, writing in 1882, con-trasted the certainties of the Benthamite school with the perplexed state of mind of Liberals of his own day: 'We shall need to see great schools before we can make sure of powerful parties.' The jurist Sir Henry Maine admired the Benthamites for their insistence that politics was a science ('they suggested and moulded the entire legislation of the fifty years just expired'), and regretted that in a democratic age it was most unlikely that a scientific conception could again exert such influence. And his fellow jurist A. V. Dicey argued that Benthamism was the dom-inant and authoritative influence on legislation in the period 1825–70, when its teaching was clear and unclouded by doubt; but that its influence waned when its followers became 'infected with candour and eclecticism'.[7] The last quarter of the century, since the demise of Benthamism, had witnessed, wrote Dicey, 'that singular phenomenon which is best described as the disintegration of beliefs or, in other words, the breaking up of established creeds, whether religious, moral, political, or economical'.[8] The history of ideas promised to yield a solution to just that disintegration of beliefs.

Another definitional difficulty facing the student of modern political thought relates to the notion of 'the political'. One reason why the renewal of the study of the history of political thought has been concentrated in the early modern period is that in that period 'political thought' possesses a clearer and more stable identity. In the middle ages the idea of 'politics' as an autonomous form of activity barely existed, while in the late modern period – from the era of the French Revolution onwards – the birth of ideology and the rise of the social sciences together make 'political thought' look like a fragile and unstable category. We have already examined the danger of collapsing political thought into political practice; we now need to comment on the instability of the notion of 'the political' in the nineteenth century. There is a powerful and familiar thesis which holds that one characteristic feature of nineteenth-century intellectual history was the erosion of the distinctively political in favour of economic and especially sociological perspectives.[9] That thesis no longer holds the field: it has suffered from the erosion of historiographical confidence in economic and social determinism, and has been more specifically taken to task in a collection of studies aiming at the recovery of the Victorian idea of a science of politics.[10] But if we return to our overarching problematic – how did Victorian thinkers seek to re-establish some kind of authoritative intellectual system which would provide the foundation for political and social order – it seems incontestable that the most compelling solutions invoked the authority of some discipline and discursive idiom lying outside the strictly political. This is not straightforwardly a symptom of the modernity of Victorian thought: it could equally well be attributed to the Hellenistic influence on Victorian culture, to the broad concept of the polity which that influence sustained, and to the conviction that political authority could not be sharply distinguished from other kinds of social and moral authority.[11] The political was not sealed off from the ethical and the religious. We are dealing, after all, with an age in which Gladstone's first book, on the problem of ecclesiastical establishment, could be conceived as 'a book upon a portion of political science', and in which at the end of his life he could advise 'the intending politician, if of masculine and serious mind' to fortify his mind on the *Analogy of Religion*, by the eighteenth-century Anglican divine, Bishop Butler.[12] The late Victorians, in particular, were deeply resistant to what the modernist theologian Hastings Rashdall, writing in 1895, denounced as 'the naive distinction between ethics and politics'.[13] Ethical conceptions of the state reigned supreme, among both individualists and collectivists, and it was only such dissidents as the emerging school of pluralists who were content with an instrumental conception of the state, since that was something it was easy to be 'against'.

The point I am making is that the decision to frame this study in terms of the quest for an authoritative language in which politics could be discussed implies the application of a relaxed definition of the boundaries of 'political' thought. For the search for authority inevitably took thinkers beyond the realm of the political, narrowly defined, into such fields as political economy, natural science, history, ethics and theology. So a history of this endeavour has to set political thought against the background of the broader intellectual culture of Victorian Britain. That is the main purpose of this book.

1

ECONOMIC MEN: POLITICAL ECONOMY AND POLITICAL THOUGHT

In British as in European politics, the 1830s heralded a new age, marked by the invention of a political vocabulary which has pervaded political life in the west up to the present. In the years 1828–34 the British state underwent a series of reforms which, taken together, were so fundamental that some historians have seen in them the dismantling of the *ancien régime*. The confessional character of the state was abandoned in essentials as Protestant dissenters and then Roman Catholics were admitted to full political rights; the Reform Act of 1832 marked a recognition that political institutions could not remain untouched by fundamental structural change in society; and the new poor law of 1834 overturned the structures that had governed the relief of poverty since the Elizabethan age and marked a major step towards the administrative state.

The decade in which Victoria ascended the throne also saw the deaths of Bentham and Coleridge, the writers whom John Stuart Mill characterized as 'the two great seminal minds of England in their age'; and it saw the demise of a number of other important political writers such as James Mill and Godwin, Hazlitt and Cobbett. It also brought to public prominence a remarkable number of the writers who were to dominate the intellectual landscape of the first half of the Victorian age: T. B. Macaulay and J. S. Mill, Thomas Carlyle and F. D. Maurice, to name only a few of the most prominent. Perhaps it is appropriate to speak of 'the generation of 1830'.

The emergent doctrine that shaped the thinking of this generation – of its opponents as well as its adherents – was liberalism. Classical liberals

1

typically perceived that the advent of a modern commercial and industrial economy overturned old forms of social cohesion built upon ascribed social roles, prescriptive authority, and shared beliefs derived from the teachings of the churches. A new kind of social bond must therefore be forged, one based upon the spontaneous harmony of individual interests in what Adam Smith termed a system of natural liberty. Smith had perceived that the distinctive feature of a market-based society was that social relations would no longer depend upon communal solidarity but would instead be conducted on the basis of interest alone. These notions about the components of modernity were propounded most lucidly and articulately by French liberals such as Constant and Guizot; but these men were intellectual first cousins of the English liberals of the early nineteenth century, since all of them traced their intellectual ancestry back to Smith and the Scottish Enlightenment.

This liberal problematic haunted European social theory in the age of revolutions that stretched from Rousseau and Smith to Tocqueville and Marx. Was the interest of individuals sufficient to hold society together? Did it explain either why they do obey social norms (social cohesion) or why they ought to do so (political obligation)? Could the premise that government exists to further the interests of individuals furnish authoritative teaching about the limits to state action? Rousseau, Hegel and Comte were all contemptuous of the pretension to found a social theory upon individual interest. But in Britain the individualistic project came much closer to acquiring hegemony over social theory. It attracted some notable critics, as we shall see, but none of them forged a systematic social theory of the kind that developed on the continent. Political economy was, in a sense, the project of exploring the laws governing a modern commercial society, where social cohesion rested upon interest. Smith famously taught that we depend for our dinner not on the benevolence of the butcher, the brewer and the baker, but on their propensity to look to their own interest; a point endorsed by Malthus, who held that God had made 'the passion for self-love beyond comparison stronger than the passion of benevolence'.[1] A survey of Victorian political thought needs to start by unpacking the components of classical liberalism, the Victorians' most enduring contribution to the history of political thought. How far did classical liberalism in fact depend upon the project of founding a social theory on individual interest? This chapter will set out to show that Victorian 'individualism' was in fact driven much more by moralism than by atomism, if we take 'atomism' to mean the proposition that individuals and their interests are the only real element in society. To borrow a felicitous distinction, most Victorian liberals were 'organic' rather than 'inorganic' individualists: they grounded their individualism on some kind of conception of the social whole, rather than supposing 'society' to be a fiction and individuals alone to be real.[2]

Sources of Classical Liberalism

Benthamism

The first component of classical liberalism we need to consider is Benthamite utilitarianism. The reason is not that this was objectively the most important component, but that the utilitarians were central to what was, until recently, the most familiar narrative of Victorian political thought. This narrative was constructed in the late nineteenth century, when a whole range of very different writers argued that a great seismic shift had occurred in British political thought around the 1870s, when the Benthamite ascendency of the previous half-century was overturned, whether by the discovery of the doctrine of evolution or by the reception of German idealism, or by the creeping growth of collectivism. Some, like the idealists, thought this a positive development; others, like Dicey, deplored it; but the point is that later generations habitually defined their intellectual stance in relation to Benthamism. In doing so they constructed a caricature of the classical utilitarian system; and this caricature, though misleading as an historical account of early Victorian thought, also did important work in shaping the outlook of the later Victorian generations.

What then was utilitarianism? What was the extent of its influence? And what accounts for its appeal, given that most of the writings of its founder and chief theorist, Jeremy Bentham, were turgid and little read?

Considered as an abstract doctrine, the central features of utilitarianism are quite familiar. There are two crucial ones. First, man is treated as an abstract individual, not as a member of actual communities existing in time and place: it is thus an unhistorical doctrine. Secondly, the test of all institutions and all actions is their propensity to advance the public interest, considered not as something qualitatively distinct from, but as the aggregate of, private interests: 'the greatest happiness of the greatest number'. It is thus a consequentialist doctrine.

Three further implications may be noted. First, utilitarianism in this strict sense displays an indifference as between *types* of pleasure. Strictly there can be no 'higher' or 'lower' pleasures: to the utilitarian legislator, as Bentham put it, pushpin is as good as poetry. Secondly, not only does utilitarianism make no distinction between types of pleasure, but it also excludes any dynamic or temporal aspect to the utility principle. In utilitarianism strictly defined, there is no means of weighing the relative claims of a small but certain amount of immediate pleasure against the probability or possibility of a greater amount of pleasure in the future for the same individual; still less against a potentially infinitely multipliable amount of future pleasure consequent upon 'the improvement of the race'. The important thing about wants is that they should be satisfied, as far as possible; how those wants came to be created – for instance, by the manner in which previous sets of wants were satisfied or denied – is irrelevant. Finally, this kind of utilitarianism is indifferent as between individuals: each counts for one, and none for more than one.

This is how utilitarianism has generally been understood in twentieth-century Anglo-American moral philosophy and welfare economics. But it was in a markedly different form that the doctrine came to constitute an integral part of the Victorian outlook. We need now to look more carefully at how it came to be integrated into a broader synthesis. And we need to begin with the acknowledged father of the doctrine, Bentham, and at some of the tensions between his approach and that of his chief followers.

Jeremy Bentham (1748–1832) was essentially a product of the Enlightenment, a reformer who was persuaded that the perfectibility of man was a realistic objective which required only the right institutional environment for its attainment. He was, wrote F. D. Maurice in 1838, 'a philosopher emphatically of the last generation'.[3] His first important work (and the most readable), *A Fragment on Government*, was published in 1776, the year of the *Wealth of Nations*, while his *Introduction to the Principles of Morals and Legislation* appeared in the year of the French Revolution. It is both ironic and deeply misleading that he is often taken as a quintessentially nineteenth-century thinker. He was born just five years after Condorcet. The *Fragment on Government* begins with a ringing declaration of the author's aspiration to be the Newton of the moral sciences, an aspiration which places him firmly in Condorcet's company. His own age, Bentham wrote, was one in which 'knowledge is rapidly advancing towards perfection'. The natural world was teeming with 'discovery and improvement', and to these processes of discovery and improvement in the natural world corresponded 'reformation' in the moral world. 'What is known as Utilitarianism, or Philosophical Radicalism', wrote Elie Halévy, in a classic work, 'can be defined as nothing but an attempt to apply the principles of Newton to the affairs of politics and of morals'.[4] To Bentham's mind the science of society was a mechanical project.

The central doctrines of Bentham's creed were twofold, and were stated with singular convenience (though not without some ambiguity) in the opening lines of the *Introduction to the Principles of Morals and Legislation*. 'Nature', asserted Bentham, 'has placed mankind under the governance of two sovereign masters, *pain* and *pleasure*. It is for them alone to point out what we ought to do, as well as to determine what we shall do. On the one hand the standard of right and wrong, on the other the chain of causes and effects, are fastened to their throne.'[5] He combined, in other words, a hedonistic psychological assumption that human beings seek their own happiness with the normative principle that actions should be judged by their tendency to promote 'the greatest happiness of the greatest number'.

A good deal of scholarly debate about utilitarianism has been devoted to the relationship between these two tenets; much of it superfluous, since Bentham many times made it abundantly clear that he was quite aware of the distinction between 'is' and 'ought'. But even allowing Bentham's consciousness of that distinction, problems remain. Did Bentham mean that individuals, who are psychologically driven to pursue their own interests, *ought* nevertheless to pursue the general interest, even at the sacrifice of their own individual interests? Did he envisage a society of Fabian altruists, endlessly busying themselves with the affairs of others? Victorian critics of Benthamism accused it of allowing free rein to selfishness; but there is an equally plausible view that its weakness was the exact opposite, that it failed to carve out an area where individuals can legitimately give some preference to their own interests over those of the rest of humanity.

At the risk of unduly abridging an extensive scholarly controversy, it is possible to state quite briefly what seems the most plausible reading of Bentham's works. In asserting the general happiness principle, Bentham was primarily concerned not with the actions of individuals but with public policy and legislation. He always assumed that individuals were the best judges of their own happiness: in what it consisted, and by what means to pursue it. Christian principles of altruism and universal love, if generalized, would be 'destructive of society', since the survival of the race depended upon individuals looking after their own interests. Essentially a reformer of legal abuses, Bentham's chief interest was in the means by which government and legislators could ensure that the interest of individuals could be brought into conformity with the general interest; and he addressed his writings primarily to those concerned with the management of society.[6]

Recent historians of the early nineteenth century have found little support for the thesis of a Benthamite ascendancy in either legislation or ideology. Bentham's own works were little known before the 1840s, when Dumont's French digest of his key work, the *Introduction to the Principles of Morals and Legislation*, was translated into English. This was after the onset of the so-called 'revolution in government' which his works are supposed to have inspired. Furthermore, the philosophic radicals can no longer be understood as a tight-knit band of disciples possessed of a coherent creed. Ricardian economics, utilitarian jurisprudence and democratic politics formed a whole in James Mill's mind; but many Ricardians, including Ricardo himself, were anti-democrats, and a number of Benthamite jurists, notably John Austin, drew conservative conclusions from utilitarian premises.

Bentham, as we have seen, did not really aspire to the status of a general philosopher. He saw himself as a practical reformer of demonstrable abuses. It was his jurisprudential and penal ideas that attracted most attention in his lifetime; much more than his ethical works, which were little known before the 1830s.[7] That his ideas came to be inseparably linked with Ricardian economics and Hartley's associationist psychology to form one of the most imposing *isms* of the nineteenth century should be attributed not to Bentham himself, but to the true begetter of the philosophic radical creed, his close friend and popularizer, James Mill. Mill's presentation of Benthamism was instrumental in making that doctrine congenial to the early Victorians.

Mill for a long time held a gloomy and obscure place in the history of ideas. He was best known as the author of the fearsome educational experiment he imposed on his son, and as one of 'the bourgeoisie's economic apologists' from whom Marx absorbed classical economics. He was seen as no more than a disciple of Bentham and Ricardo. But in fact Mill's role was both much more important and much more creative than that. In order to understand this point we need to grasp some important distinctions, often blurred, between Ricardian economics and philosophic radicalism. Ricardian economics was an important component of philosophic radicalism, thanks especially to the influence of James Mill, but it was *not* the case that all Ricardians were philosophic radicals. If it were it would be difficult to reconcile the successful diffusion of Ricardianism with the fact that in political terms the philosophic radicals had proved to be a failure by 1840.[8] Among prominent Ricardians, J. R. McCulloch and Nassau Senior were Whigs; and Ricardo himself was no democrat, but took a moderate position on reform, favouring enfranchisement of 'all reasonable men', by which he meant all who would uphold private property.[9]

It is often assumed that the most basic shared tenet of utilitarianism and classical political economy was that both took *actual wants* as the starting point for social science. But James Mill was always too much of a puritan in outlook to look too kindly on men as they were, and he viewed Ricardian political economy as the science which would teach men to follow their *enlightened* self-interest, as opposed to their brutish desires. The triumph of political economy would replace hedonism with the virtues of thrift and self-denial. As Mill wrote in his *Fragment on Mackintosh* (1835), the principle of utility 'marshals the duties in their proper order, and will not permit mankind to be deluded, as so long as they have been, sottishly to prefer the lower to the higher good, and to hug the greater evil, from fear of the less'.[10] 'Wants' were arbitrary and capricious, and their sway provided no basis for social harmony. 'Interests', properly understood, were altogether more rational. Thus even in James Mill we can detect the seeds of the very un-hedonistic concern with 'character' that pervaded the moral discourse of the Victorians.

In order to understand the place of utilitarianism in the emergent doctrine of classical liberalism we therefore need to cast our net more widely, and trace its complex relationship with Whiggism. As a tradition of political thought, Whiggism characteristically sought protection for liberty in a mixed constitution in which different powers and social forces counterbalanced each other, whereas utilitarians preferred a clearly defined locus of sovereignty. Whig arguments typically rested on history, whereas utilitarians relied more on deductive reasoning. But classical liberalism owed a great deal to Whiggism, and especially to that variety of Whiggism which traced its intellectual lineage back via the *Edinburgh Review* to Adam Smith and the Scottish Enlightenment.

The 'System of the North': Adam Smith and his Legacy

One of the central arguments of this chapter will be that political doctrines founded on classical political economy were much more complex and more diverse than is often thought. In part this was because of change over time: J. S. Mill and his generation substantially modified the liberalism of the early utilitarians. But it is important to recognize that the complexity was present in classical liberalism from the outset. Just as Benthamism was marked by a tension between self-interest and the general good, so a tension between 'wealth' and 'virtue' pervaded Adam Smith's thinking, rather than serving to characterize the distinction between his outlook and that of his critics. No more in Smith than in Bentham was the harmony of interests unproblematical. For Smith never believed that a 'system of natural liberty' could generate a spontaneous harmony of interests without a proper framework of political institutions. Of course he believed that social and economic progress sprang from the individual's self-interested pursuit of wealth; but he also warned of the dangers that government, which was necessary to furnish a framework of security by means of the provision of justice and defence, might be subverted by particular interests. Whereas landowners and labourers, he held, had interests which were naturally coincident with the general interest of society, the same was not true of the other main interest in society, that of 'employers of stock', or capitalists. Merchants and manufacturers, according to Smith, had an interest in persuading government to grant them a range of privileges and monopolies which were antagonistic to the general interest. And he doubted whether landowners or labourers naturally possessed the civic spirit which would enable them to stand up to the capitalist interest. Smith believed, as Hume had done, that commercial society, by generating abundance, would make universal citizenship possible: the civic rights of the few need no longer rest upon the subordination of the many, as they had in the ancient republics. But social and political institutions had to be developed which would foster an ethos of devotion to the common good, for Smith recognized that the functional specialization which was an inseparable component of the division of labour tended to promote mental narrowness and torpidity, at least in the labouring classes. The market carried with it the promise of plenty, which would make universal citizenship attainable; but it also threatened to erode that very devotion to the public good which constituted the substance of citizenship. Smith thus posed one of the central dilemmas of modern political theory.

Smith 'solved' the difficulty by two principal means. First, he accorded an important role to the educational system in fostering the mental and moral qualities required of the citizens. Generally speaking, Smith was opposed to the provision of education at the public expense, since he thought it encouraged idleness on the part of the teachers, who could be given an incentive to hard work and efficient performance of their duties only if they were directly dependent upon their pupils for their income. But he made an exception for the provision of primary education for the 'common people'. And for all levels of society he favoured the institution of incentives to education in the form of educational qualifications for entry into various kinds of trades, professions and employment. In addition, the common people were to be compelled to undertake compulsory military exercises on the Greek or Roman model, since these could help counteract the 'mental mutilation' consequent upon the division of labour.

Secondly, Smith held that oppressive government (which could be a fatal obstacle to economic development) could best be prevented not by 'republican' means (citizen militias, for example, instead of standing armies) but by the principles of parliamentary sovereignty and taxation by representative consent. The large and civilized monarchical states of modern Europe, which he admired in a number of respects, were nevertheless defective in their reliance upon an oppressive and wasteful system of public finance. It was British government that constituted something like the model of free government in a commercial society. Smith thus sketched a synthesis of free-market economics with two of the other key pillars of Victorian political thought: the newly emergent doctrine of parliamentary sovereignty and the notion of education for citizenship.

But how did Smith's ideas come to be absorbed into the mainstream of early nineteenth-century English political thought? This process has been illuminated recently by scholars such as Winch and Fontana, whose work has convincingly demonstrated that political economy, far from being a monopoly of the philosophic radicals, in fact had strong Whiggish connections.

Dugald Stewart (1753–1828), Professor of Moral Philosophy at the University of Edinburgh from 1785 to 1810, was a key figure in bringing Smith's influence to bear upon the Whig tradition, and transmitting it into the mainstream of Victorian liberalism. Not himself a great original mind, Stewart was a great educator who instilled into a generation of young literary intellectuals a distinctive intellectual temperament which would characterize the *Edinburgh Review* at its zenith. In his lectures at Edinburgh he placed political economy within the 'common sense' and intuitionist philosophical tradition. These lectures became available to the wider public only in the 1850s, so it is clear that Stewart's influence was exerted personally over his pupils. But he held his chair at a time when it was fashionable for young Whig noblemen to complete their education at Edinburgh, and these pupils included a galaxy of future Whig politicians and publicists: Palmerston, Russell, Lansdowne, Lauderdale, the Earl of Dudley and Alexander Baring (Lord Ashburton), as well as the *Edinburgh* reviewers Jeffrey, Horner and Brougham. Sir James Mackintosh too was a close friend of Stewart's.

Stewart's pupils further disseminated 'Scottish philosophy' through such agencies as the *Encyclopaedia Britannica*, the Society for the Diffusion of Useful Knowledge, and the University of London. But it was the *Edinburgh Review* – founded in 1802, and edited until 1829 by Jeffrey – that played a decisive role in the transmission of 'the system of the north' into metropolitan culture. A decade or so after its foundation it had attained a circulation of some thirteen thousand, and was a formative influence on British intellectual culture in the early nineteenth century, largely due to Jeffrey's success in grouping around him a galaxy of talented writers.

The best-known literary figure in this circle was Thomas Babington Macaulay, who was recruited as a reviewer in 1825 and made his name with a series of blistering reviews, whose victims included James Mill, Southey and the young Gladstone. Macaulay was educated at Cambridge, not at Edinburgh, and so absorbed the Scottish philosophy at second hand, but when he entered parliament in 1830 it was as the member for the pocket borough of Calne, thanks to its patron, Stewart's pupil Lord Lansdowne. In the Commons Macaulay laid the foundations of a political reputation through the speeches he made in support of parliamentary reform, for he made the case on the basis of an historical argument which was typical of *Edinburgh Review* Whiggism. The old electoral system was unworkable, he argued, not because of any inherent absurdity or injustice, but because the progress of society, especially the rise of commercial society, made new political forms necessary. This argument owed something to an older strand in the Whig tradition which maintained that liberty was not an ancient possession but a modern achievement. Furthermore, Macaulay's argument was not that the commercial and industrial middle class must henceforth be dominant, as James Mill argued; but rather it constituted a growing social force which must be recognized by the electoral system so as to restore the balance of the constitution.

The Scottish school decisively shifted the focus of political theory away from questions of legitimacy and the grounds of obligation. Their idea of scientific politics implied a gradualist view of politics, which proceeded 'not by delineating plans of new constitutions, but by enlightening the policy of actual legislators'. For one of the main conclusions of the new science of politics was that 'the happiness of mankind depends, not on the share which the people possess, directly or indirectly, in the enactment of laws, but on the equity and expedience of the laws that are enacted'.[11] What was important was not the form of government but 'the particular system of *law and policy* which that form introduces'. Political economy – the science which was 'most immediately connected with human happiness and improvement' – could, according to Stewart, be 'studied without reference to constitutional forms – not only because the tendency of laws may be investigated abstractly from all considerations of their origin but because there are many principles of political economy which may be sanctioned by governments very different in their constitutions'.[12]

In their approach to political institutions these Scots had a marked preference for a historically based approach over deductive and *a priori* political theory. The Scottish philosophers and historians regarded society not as an artefact, but as an entity that evolved in ways that transcended human design. Forms of government were not good or bad in the abstract, but only in relation to the particular kind of society they sought to govern. The study of institutions was thus dependent upon a 'conjectural history' of the development of civilization, which sought to demarcate distinct 'stages of society' and the forms of government that corresponded to them. At the heart of the Scots' inquiry, then, was a search for the forms of government most appropriate for commercial societies.

On the face of things, a philosophical chasm separated the Edinburgh Whigs from the philosophic radicals. The philosophical tradition represented by Stewart was deeply alien to Bentham, who dismissed common sense as a euphemism for unreasoning prejudice; and the philosophic radicals set up their own organ, the *Westminster Review*, as a rival to the *Edinburgh*. The historicism of the *Edinburgh Review*, furthermore, sits uneasily alongside the abstractly unhistorical approach commonly attributed to the Benthamites. But the relationship between the two traditions was not as antagonistic as first impressions might suggest. James Mill, who more than any other man was responsible for shaping Bentham's ideas into a political creed, was himself a pupil of Dugald Stewart; and Mill professed that it was to Stewart that he owed 'the taste for the studies which have formed my favourite pursuits, and which will be so till the end of my life'.[13] John Stuart Mill told Comte that his father was 'the last survivor' of the Scottish school. Bentham's Genevan editor, Etienne Dumont, was in contact with the London Whigs and was one of those responsible for disseminating the ideas of the Scottish philosophers in the French-speaking world. When the *Edinburgh Review* published Macaulay's attack on James Mill, its editor was MacVey Napier, who had himself been responsible for commissioning Mill's original *Essay on Government* for the *Encyclopaedia Britannica*. Like Mill, Napier was a former pupil of Dugald Stewart.

In general, Edinburgh Whigs and philosophic radicals were in substantial agreement on a wide range of practical issues, but disagreed over the philosophical foundations. In private ethics, for instance, Whigs recognized that the pursuit of personal happiness was an important component of human motivation, but they preferred to see this as an historical fact about commercial society and its values, and not as a universal truth about human nature. In public ethics, Whigs were as clear as philosophic radicals that the end of government was the promotion of happiness rather than virtue or right religion. Macaulay admonished the young Gladstone for supposing government to be 'an institution for the propagation of religion': Gladstone's system would, he thought, compromise government's 'primary end', which Macaulay took to be 'the protection of the persons and the property of men'.[14] Macaulayesque Whigs shared the utilitarian conception of government as a necessary evil, contrived by men for the avoidance of greater evils. Lord Melbourne, who of all Whig statesmen was least inclined to a 'high' view of government, pronounced that the state existed merely 'to prevent crime and to preserve contracts'. And though Bentham was the most anti-Whig of all the utilitarians, Whigs found little difficulty in accepting much of his jurisprudence. Whigs could agree with much of philosophic radicalism as a practical reform programme for commercial society.

The Whigs' criticisms of philosophic radicals were twofold. They saw the theoretical basis of utilitarianism as crude and unhistorical, and preferred the historical and inductive method to the utilitarians' fondness for the deductive method. They did not see in utilitarianism a credible general philosophy, and dissented from its hedonistic psychological assumptions and its historically unsophisticated conception of human nature. Few utilitarians before J. S. Mill had the Edinburgh Whigs' sense of the ways in which different types of society produced different value systems. Secondly, and practically, Whigs disliked the democratic principles championed by the later Bentham, and instead defended the notion of a mixed constitution and historically based legitimacy. These notions were articulated notably by Sir James Mackintosh in his attack on Bentham's *Plan of Parliamentary Reform* (1817). Mackintosh argued that the existing variety of suffrages and types of constituency – which utilitarians denounced as an irrational hotchpotch – should not be simplified but extended and broadened, so as to incorporate the range of different interests existing in the nation.

James Mill was a noted critic of the Whig theory of government. He denounced its class theory of representation, which would merely replace a pure aristocracy with 'a motley Aristocracy'. The Whig theory of government was, he thought, 'an operose contrivance to insure bad government', 'a mere folly'.[15] Mill's *Essay on Government*, which argued that a representative system based on universal adult male suffrage was the only system capable of securing good government, could be read as a thinly disguised attack on the theory of the mixed constitution. That was why it provoked Macaulay into one of his most brilliant pieces of polemical writing. Significantly, he focused on Mill's method, which seemed to him resolutely deductive and unhistorical: 'Our objection to the Essay of Mr Mill is fundamental. We believe that it is utterly imposs-ible to deduce the science of government from the principles of human nature.'[16]

Yet in a sense the polemic between Macaulay and Mill, though framed in fundamental terms, was rather like a family quarrel. Macaulay accepted that he and Mill shared the common premise 'that the end of govern-ment was to produce the greatest happiness of mankind'.[17] When, later in life, Macaulay came to compile his collected essays, he chose not to include his review of Mill. He explained that though he still stood by his analysis of the defects of Mill's *Essay*, he now believed that 'a critic, while noticing those faults, should have abstained from using contemptuous language respecting the historian of British India'. He thought Mill's *History* 'on the whole, the greatest historical work which has appeared in our language since that of Gibbon'. Macaulay was puzzled as to how Mill could advocate the application of deductive methods in studying the political institutions of his own time and country, when as a historian he used a very different method to great effect. How could Mill combine the 'Scottish' interest in conjectural history with his attachment to deductive methods and the assumption that action is governed by self-interest? For Macaulay it was precisely because the history of society was (as the Scots insisted) a history of progress that political science must necessarily be progressive and experimental.

Malthus

Both Edinburgh Whiggism and Benthamite utilitarianism were children of the Enlightenment, which may be why these two apparently alien creeds were able to forge an alliance. But in European rather than simply British terms there are good grounds for arguing that the originality of early nineteenth-century social thought fed on a Janus-faced relationship with the Enlightenment and the French Revolution. In the British case this argument can best be exemplified by considering Thomas Robert Malthus, a pre-Victorian thinker whose broad and profound impact on the early Victorian outlook is beyond question. The central features of the Malthusian system are well enough known. In the work that made his name, the *Essay on the Principle of Population* of 1798, he maintained that an 'imminent and immediate' tendency for population growth to outstrip the food supply placed severe limits on the prospects of any long-term improvement in working-class living standards above subsistence level. This doctrine, soon absorbed into the classical system, earned political economy the epithet 'the dismal science', for it seemed to teach that poverty was the normal condition of the mass of the population. But the broader significance of Malthus's work is open to dispute.

Two quite distinct interpretations of Malthus present themselves in the scholarly literature. Some view him as a child of the Enlightenment, but to others his intellectual stance seems to mark a radical break with Adam Smith and with Anglo-Scottish intellectual Whiggery. Some commentators, such as the historian of economic thought, Samuel Hollander, see Malthus as an optimist and a reformer; others, notably Gertrude Himmelfarb, have argued quite vociferously that he was in fact deeply pessimistic about prospects for social improvement. Himmelfarb indeed maintains that the *Essay on Population* was 'revolutionary in relation to the *Wealth of Nations* itself', and that 'it is hard to imagine a more thorough reversal of thought, short of a return to mercantilism'.[18] My own argument is that this polarization of scholarly debate betokens a genuine and creative ambiguity at the heart of Malthus's work. For an ambivalent relationship with the Enlightenment was wholly characteristic of the most fertile and original European social thinkers of the post-revolutionary period: writers such as Saint-Simon and Comte, Hegel and Mazzini.

Malthus certainly had deep roots in the Enlightenment, although this is not always recognized. There is a popular image of 'Parson Malthus' as a man nurtured at the bosom of the Anglican Establishment, the friend of country gentlemen and the ally of the agrarian interest. Thus pictured, he seems remote from the traditions of intellectual inquiry inherited from the Enlightenment. The French Revolution and the prolonged period of warfare precipitated an upper- and middle-class reaction against the supposed intellectual sources of 'Jacobinism'.[19] But this picture sits rather uneasily beside much else that we know of Malthus. His father, who was indeed a country gentleman, was a man of decidedly unorthodox intellectual tastes who had a particular enthusiasm for the works of Rousseau. Malthus's own education was by no means a conventional clerical one. Before going up to Cambridge he was educated – unusually for a person of his social class – by the leading unitarian controversialist Gilbert Wakefield at the Dissenting Academy at Warrington. Malthus always saw himself as a Whig; and at times his stance was that of an advanced Whig. His support for Catholic emancipation and for the removal of dissenters' public disabilities clearly identified him with that party. He was indeed close to a number of the founders of the *Edinburgh Review*, and this leading Whig periodical backed his population doctrines wholeheartedly. Towards the end of his life he was to write on political economy for the Tory *Quarterly Review*; but this was only after his support for the corn laws, and his adumbration of underconsumptionist doctrines, had enabled the Ricardians to marginalize him.

Furthermore, contrary to Himmelfarb's argument, Malthus's work on political economy continued to be couched within the framework of a largely eighteenth-century inquiry into the consequences of the growth of commercial society. In an unpublished pamphlet of 1796 he opposed Pittite repression, and called for an alliance of country gentlemen and middle classes to revive 'true Whig principles' and mediate between the ministry and the popular radicals. This was a synthesis of 'country Whiggism' – the belief that the main threat to English liberties came from the growth of executive power, and that country gentlemen were the main bulwark against the excesses of that power – with a 'modern Whig' faith in the emergent middle classes as an alternative source of support for English liberties. In a sense this heralded some of the main themes of Malthus's mature thought, for the extent of his 'agrarianism', or antagonism towards commercial and manufacturing interests, is liable to be exaggerated. He was fully conscious of the potential social and political benefits of economic growth. His anxiety, reflected in his support for the corn laws, focused on the dangers inherent in Britain's tendency to

import a growing proportion of her food needs, and the growing imbal-
ance between agriculture on the one hand and commerce and manufacturing on the other.

On the other hand it is evident that the pessimism apparent in the
Essay, especially in its first edition, was induced by reaction against the
French Revolution. Malthus himself made it clear that the radical egalitar-
ianism of Godwin and Condorcet was his chief target. As he commented
on Condorcet's speculation as to the possibility of indefinite progress
with respect to the duration of human life, 'if this be the case, there is at
once an end to all human science' and 'the wildest and most improbable
conjectures may be advanced with as much certainty as the most just and
sublime theories founded on careful and reiterated experiment'. For
'the constancy of the laws of nature and of effects and causes, is the
foundation of all human knowledge'.[20] Malthus's unwavering attachment to the application of what he took to be Newtonian methods to the
moral and social sciences showed the depth of his commitment to the
Enlightenment project.

The point is that it was precisely his roots in Enlightenment traditions
of inquiry that made Malthus such a powerful controversialist in opposition to revolutionary utopianism. Indeed, it is clear from the passages
quoted above that what appalled him about the speculations of such
men as Godwin and Condorcet was precisely that they seemed to be
betraying the soberly scientific outlook that Malthus so prized in the
Enlightenment. The importance of the *Essay*, then, was that it did
indeed form part of the conservative response to the French Revolution,
but that, unlike Burke (whose work was as alien to him as Godwin's was),
Malthus was able to mobilize a quasi-scientific authority behind the conservative cause.[21] It was that quasi-scientific authority, together with the
markedly more reformist tone of the second *Essay*, which made Malthusianism, in spite of its conservative affinities, so appealing to such
men as Bentham, Ricardo and J. S. Mill.

Malthus was in fact never more than at most a moderate pessimist. He
wished to discredit the boundless and in his view unscientific optimism
of the radical egalitarians, but he had no wish to undercut the cause of
scientifically grounded reform. It was only in the absence of prudential
restraint that the path of wages was inevitably downwards. Malthus
came increasingly to stress a point that was already present in the 1798
edition of the *Essay*, namely the possibility that a taste for 'conveniences
and comforts' on the part of the labouring classes might generate
prudential habits which were capable of checking the population growth

rate without the necessity of 'misery'. That was why Malthus insisted, towards the end of his life, that 'the general and practical conclusions which I have myself drawn from my principles both on population and rent, have by no means the gloomy aspect given to them by many of my readers';[22] and why J. S. Mill asserted, paradoxically, that it was only from the time of Malthus onwards that 'the economical condition of the labouring classes [has] been regarded by thoughtful men as susceptible of permanent improvement'.[23]

Malthus was, of course, an Anglican divine, and his political economy had its roots in the fashionable natural theology of the time. If 'self-love' was, as he thought, integral to the operation of the social mechanism, this was in accord with the sort of theological utilitarianism taught by William Paley. What has become abundantly clear in recent years is that, though Malthus's demographic ideas were rapidly absorbed into secular political economy, the brand of Christian economics he typified also flourished at the outset of the Victorian period. We need to turn to this tradition now in order to obtain a sense of the diverse ideological affinities of political economy in the early nineteenth century.

Christian Political Economy

A generation ago, much scholarly energy was devoted to the question of the influence of ideology upon the 'revolution in government' in the mid-nineteenth century; though the debate was confused by uncertainty about the character of the transformations that were being explained. By ideology, however, was meant Benthamite utilitarianism; the assumption was that no Tory could have been a true believer in political economy, and that the Liberal Tories – men such as Huskisson who spearheaded the drive towards free trade in the 1820s – had simply capitulated to the spirit of the age. The debate has been much illuminated by recent work which has shown just how misleading is the picture of a pitched battle between secular, scientific, utilitarian political economy on the one hand and its evangelical or High Tory critics on the other. Ideology did indeed shape the 'revolution in government' of 1820–50, as such measures as the liberalization of trade and the reform of the poor law transformed the nature of British government. But the key to that ideological influence was not the fusion of Benthamite utilitarianism and Ricardian political economy that we know as philosophic radicalism. Instead, the chief influence was a Christian political economy whose policy prescriptions (*laissez-faire* and the suppression of outdoor relief)

dovetailed neatly with those of classical economics, though its foundations were very different. While classical economics of the Smith–Ricardo
line of descent had an important influence on the Whigs, especially the
Edinburgh Review circle, and also on the radicals of the Anti-Corn Law
League, Christian political economy entered the world of public policy
chiefly through the agency of Liberal Tories such as Huskisson and Peel.
Laissez-faire and political economy did not form a monolithic bloc, and
a distinction needs to be drawn between, in Boyd Hilton's words, 'an
evangelical, backward-looking pessimism' which 'developed in a context
of piety and pessimism' and 'growth-oriented optimism' whose context
was a passion for science, improvement and useful knowledge.[24] Whigs
and Liberal Tories could agree on many practical questions of economic
policy; but if they shared a belief in *laissez-faire* this was not because of a
common attachment to secular liberalism. Where Whigs tended to be
enthused by the cause of 'improvement', Liberal Tories rested their economic liberalism on an evangelical pessimism that discounted the possibility of continuing progress in this world.

The key intellectual influence upon Christian political economy was
the Scottish evangelical preacher Thomas Chalmers, whom Malthus
regarded as his 'ablest and best ally'.[25] Formerly seen as a paternalist,
Chalmers has recently come to be reinterpreted as a rather doctrinaire
adherent of *laissez-faire* individualism. His outlook was founded upon
what Hilton terms a moderate evangelical theodicy (or model of the
operation of divine providence in the world): for Chalmers, providence
operates, so to speak, mechanically, the world being so designed that
suffering is the natural and predictable consequence of sin and improvidence. The main theological source of this theodicy was the eighteenth-
century prelate and theologian Joseph Butler – a major influence on
early Victorian intellectual history – who had developed a model of a
system of natural rewards and punishments. But it was probably Malthus's population principle which suggested the application of this theology to social and economic thought. Workers' procreation (as opposed
to the exercise of moral restraint and providence counselled by Malthus
in his second essay) would lead inevitably to overpopulation and hence
to falling wage levels and to starvation. In the same way capitalist speculation would lead inexorably to gluts and hence to crisis and bankruptcy.
For evangelicals such as Chalmers, Malthusianism thus revealed a providential moral discipline at work in the economic order.

This mechanical conception of the operation of providence was logic-
ally related to support for *laissez-faire*. Man-made laws such as protective

tariffs or indiscriminate 'outdoor relief' for the poor tended to obstruct the operation of this natural system of rewards and punishments. Moderate evangelicals such as Chalmers and Wilberforce were dedicated free traders, and supporters of the new poor laws; they opposed the introduction of factory legislation which was sponsored by men such as Shaftesbury. Shaftesbury, though often taken as a representative evangelical (hence the picture of evangelical opposition to *laissez-faire*) in fact personified an alternative evangelical theodicy ('extremist', according to Hilton) in which providence worked not naturally but miraculously. If the moderate theodicy underpinned the economic policies of the Liberal Tories, the extremist version appealed to traditional Tory paternalists as well as to those oddballs whom historians label Tory radicals.

The understanding of the nature of Christian political economy has been applied to the problem of the ideological origins of the revolution in government in the on-going debate on the origins of the new poor law of 1834. The act of 1834 is often taken as a quintessentially Benthamite piece of legislation. The principle of 'less eligibility' (support for the able-bodied poor should be available only in the workhouse, where conditions must be made 'less eligible' than those for the poor outside, for otherwise the working class would prefer reliance on public assistance to self-reliance) was thought to be rooted in the mechanically hedonistic psychology of the utilitarians. But Mandler has pointed out the deep implausibility of viewing the new poor law as 'an alien imposition by Benthamite bureaucrats': if that is what it was, why should the landed gentry, who exercised power in the counties, have implemented a measure which was such an affront to landed values?[26] Most of the assistant commissioners who did the bulk of the work for the 1834 act were from 'the political cream of the landed élite'; and, Mandler suggests, 'this élite within the landed élite was not only familiar with, but absolutely saturated by, Christian versions of political economy by 1830'.[27] It is only by invoking the influence of Christian political economy that we can explain why, for instance, the High Tory and High Churchman J. W. Croker, who thought that utilitarianism would reduce society to 'a fortuitous concourse of atoms', could defend the new poor law of 1834 against its detractors.[28] Conversely, one of the most prominent theoretical opponents of the new poor law was the Ricardian McCulloch.[29]

The debate about the relationship between ideology and the 'revolution in government' has been clouded, then, by a confusion of two claims. The claim that measures such as the 1834 Poor Law Amendment Act were the product of a coherent and cohesive band of Benthamite or

Ricardian ideologues is clearly no longer tenable. Mandler is surely right to ask how such a measure could have been implemented, given the way in which rural England continued to be governed. But this is not enough to refute a second claim: that the new poor law cannot be explained in terms of pragmatic response to events, without reference to social thought. 'Agreement is reached', wrote Halévy, who remains a sure guide in such matters, 'as much on the programme of practical applications as on the principles';[30] and the important point is that, on questions such as poor law reform and free trade, classical and Christian political economists reached substantially the same conclusions, whatever their differences on fundamentals. The new poor law could not have been successfully implemented had it not won enthusiastic support from the more educated of the landed gentry; while, conversely, the Whigs in government arguably owed less to Christian political economy, which had its greatest following among Liberal Tories, than to its secular counterpart.

The rediscovery of the vitality of Christian political economy has thoroughly discredited the old and plausible bipolar image of early Victorian thought, in which utilitarians and Manchesterite radicals reigned supreme, and were combated only by an assorted band of philosophical idealists (Coleridge and Carlyle) and Tory romantics (Southey and Disraeli). What Hilton and others offer is a portrait of a more or less intellectually coherent Liberal Toryism, personified by such men as Huskisson and Peel, which was far from the unprincipled capitulation to utilitarian liberalism depicted in Disraeli's critique. The central point about Victorian liberalism is that its assumptions were absorbed into the mainstream and were embraced by Conservatives as much as by party Liberals, so that the Ricardian and *Edinburgh* reviewer McCulloch could act as economic advisor to Conservative Prime Minister Peel in the 1840s. That was what distinguished the fortunes of liberalism in England from its fortunes in continental Europe; and Hilton's is by far the most convincing account yet offered of how that happened. Conservative responses to political economy, therefore, were by no means only negative or opportunistic. Nevertheless there was an intellectually significant tradition of cultural critiques of political economy; a tradition which was mainly but not exclusively conservative. That tradition now needs to be examined.

Critics of Political Economy

Recent focus on Christian political economy should not blind us to the existence of a powerful, and mainly Tory, current of opposition to the market economy and the classical economists. Often this was rooted in the belief that market capitalism was innately cosmopolitan: as the Tory Radical Richard Oastler asked, 'in what age or nation was a capitalist known to be a Patriot?' Likewise an Ultra-Tory newspaper accused the economists of having discovered 'that patriotism was nonsense'.[31] Other Tories such as Croker engaged more directly with the concerns of political economy, and instead of dismissing the discipline as a whole, set out to challenge its free-trade bias. Their case for protectionism was not a simple obscurantist reflex, but consisted of a subtle blend of economic and constitutional arguments. A regime of protection, so they argued, sustained social cohesion by encouraging sectoral diversity and preventing over-specialization. But it also stood at the heart of the constitutional order, for it allowed governments the latitude to ensure that public policy represented the breadth of interests of the propertied classes.[32]

Of all the various cultural critics of political economy and individualism the most intellectually important was Samuel Taylor Coleridge. Coleridge was only very ambiguously a conservative, being a pioneer of biblical criticism and non-doctrinal Christianity, and thus a forerunner of an important strand within Victorian liberalism. Mill and Maurice both noted that Coleridge's intellectual appeal, especially to conservatives, was much greater after his death than in his lifetime. Some subsequent commentators on the conservative tradition have been inclined to dispute Coleridge's place in it, on the grounds that he was no political sceptic and that his idealism was doubtfully compatible with conservatism.[33] But he was certainly no friend of the utilitarians or the classical economists, and his antagonism to Malthus in particular long predated his turn to conservatism. In his *Lay Sermon* of 1817 he attributed contemporary evils to an 'overbalance of the commercial spirit'; and he contemptuously dismissed political economy as a 'pretended science' and a 'Humbug', which substituted 'the guess-work of general consequences' for 'moral and political philosophy'.[34] He found in political economy 'a multitude of sophisms but not a single just and important result which might not be far more convincingly deduced from the simplest principles of morality and common sense'.[35] Instead Coleridge, who had imbibed the ideas of the German idealists and romantics, invoked 'the science of HISTORY – History studied in the light of philosophy, as the great drama of an ever unfolding Providence – [which] infuses hope and reverential thoughts of man and his destination'.

J. S. Mill, who found much to admire in Coleridge's mind, was nevertheless dismissive of Coleridge's economic writings: 'in political economy ... he writes like an arrant driveller, and it would have been well for his reputation had he never meddled with the subject'.[36] In fact Coleridge had some interesting and subtle views to offer, notably a critique of 'narcotic bullionists' who took the return to the gold standard as the touchstone of economic truth. But Mill was right in the sense that it is not primarily on his economic ideas that Coleridge's reputation as a social theorist rests. He perceived that the weakness of utilitarian liberalism was that it could give no plausible account of either cultural authority or social cohesion; and it was to supply those gaps that he developed his theory of nationality. He insisted, for instance, upon the representation of interests, not individuals, as the proper constitutional principle. 'The miserable tendency of all [schemes of parliamentary reform]', he maintained, 'is to destroy our nationality, which consists, in a principal degree, in our representative government, and to convert it into a degrading delegation of the populace. There is no unity for a people but in a representation of national interests; a delegation from the passions or wishes of the individuals themselves is a rope of sand.'[37] There were, he insisted, two great *orders* in the state: the landed and the personal; and to them corresponded the two great *interests* in the state, *permanence* and *progression*.

Coleridge made a rhetorical move of great importance for Victorian political thought when he elevated the idea of the 'national' and made it the polar opposite of the partial and the provincial. He was contemptuous of the cultural institutions of provincial dissent: Lancasterian schools, mechanics' institutes, and 'lecture bazaars under the absurd name of universities'. They were no substitute for 'a permanent, nationalized, learned order, a national clerisy or Church is an essential element of a rightly constituted nation'.

His most important work of political theory, the *Constitution of Church and State*, was an extended argument to show that a modern society could not rest exclusively upon commerce, but that the commercial interest, representing progress, must be balanced by a stabilizing interest in the form of landed property; and that it must be disciplined by the endowment of a clerisy whose responsibility was the perpetuation of culture.

What utilitarians and evangelical political economists had in common was, above all, a mechanical cast of mind; and perhaps the most acute critic of that cast of mind was Thomas Carlyle, who was also the most famous of all the Victorian critics of political economy. In an early essay he characterized his own age as an 'Age of Machinery', by which he meant not just a manufacturing age, but an age whose entire intellectual culture was pervaded by a mechanical spirit. Even politics was reduced to a mechanism, and civil government termed 'the Machine of Society'. Likewise the preoccupation with institutional reform was a symptom of a mechanically minded age. Carlyle lamented the demise of metaphysics and the moral sciences, and argued that 'there is a science of *Dynamics* in man's fortunes and nature, as well as of *Mechanics*'. Human affairs could not be understood by the methods of political economy, which focused exclusively on the mechanical aspect of society.[38]

Carlyle was the most incisive critic of the sociological plausibility of 'Benthamee Radicalism, or the gospel of "Enlightened Selfishness"';[39] under which heading he included both utilitarian ethics and jurisprudence, and classical political economy. This whole system failed, he thought, because it could offer no plausible account of social cohesion. This critique was articulated in three key works, *Sartor Resartus* (1833), *Chartism* (1839), and *Past and Present* (1843). In the first Carlyle expounded his cyclical conception of history: excoriating contemporary society as a society in decay, he at the same time prophesied renewal and regeneration. Speaking through the voice of Herr Teufelsdröckh he maintained that, in the absence of any 'Social Idea', society stood on the point of extinction. The church was 'fallen speechless, from obesity and apoplexy', and the state was 'shrunken into a Police-Office, straitened to get its pay'.

The Soul Politic having departed, what can follow but that the Body Politic be decently interred, to avoid putrescence? Liberals, Economists, Utilitarians enough I see marching with its bier, and chanting loud paeans, towards the funeral-pile, where, amid wailings from some, and saturnalian revelries from the most, the venerable Corpse is to be burnt. Or, in plain words, that these men, Liberals, Utilitarians, or whatsoever they are called, will ultimately carry their point, and dissever and destroy most existing Institutions of Society, seems a thing which has some time ago ceased to be doubtful.

Even amidst the conflagration, Teufelsdröckh was convinced, religion was 'weaving for herself new Vestures'; and 'the golden age, which a blind tradition has hitherto placed in the Past, is Before us'.[40]

In *Chartism* and *Past and Present* Carlyle was chiefly concerned to assert his belief in man's essential need to be governed. If the key tenet of early Victorian individualism was the belief that individuals are the best judges of their own interests, Carlyle was its most articulate critic. He deemed *laissez-faire* 'as good as an *abdication* on the part of governors; an admission that they are henceforth incompetent to govern, that they are not there to govern at all'.[41] He was dismissive of the notion that the English people of his age lived a life in *society*, in the proper sense. Just as the French counterrevolutionaries Maistre and Bonald held that a society founded on the principles of 1789 was no society at all, so Carlyle thought that free-trade liberalism was mining the foundations of social order. 'Our life is not a mutual helpfulness; but rather, cloaked under due laws-of-war, named "fair competition" and so forth, it is a mutual hostility. We have profoundly forgotten everywhere that *Cash-payment* is not the sole relation of human beings; we think, nothing doubting, that *it* absolves and liquidates all engagements of man.'[42]

His core belief was that 'man has a soul in him, *different* from the stomach in any sense of this word'; and he lambasted the utilitarians for confusing soul and stomach. He deplored the spiritual emptiness of the age. 'God's absolute Laws, sanctioned by an eternal Heaven and an eternal Hell, have become Moral Philosophies, sanctioned by able computations of Profit and Loss, by weak considerations of Pleasures of Virtue and the Moral Sublime. . . . We quietly believe this Universe to be intrinsically a great unintelligible PERHAPS. . . . God's Laws are become a Greatest-Happiness Principle, a Parliamentary Expediency.'[43] As a theologian Carlyle was dismissive of Paley and the natural theology tradition. 'The ALMIGHTY MAKER is not like a Clockmaker that once, in old immemorial ages, having *made* his Horologe of a Universe, sits ever since and sees it go! Not at all. Hence comes Atheism . . . . For the faith in an Invisible, Unnameable, Godlike, present everywhere in all that we see and work and suffer, is the essence of all faith whatever.'

Carlyle was an expert debunker of the emerging pieties of the Victorian age. He dismissed the classical liberal definition of liberty, or 'negative liberty', as it has become known; for him, the proper definition of liberty must be derivative of truth and right. 'Liberty?', he asked: 'The true liberty of a man, you would say, consisted in his finding out, or being forced to find out the right path, and to walk thereon. To learn, or to be taught, what work he actually was able for; and then by permission, persuasion, and even compulsion, to set about doing of the same! That is his true blessedness, honour, "liberty" and maximum of wellbeing: if liberty be not that, I for one have small care about liberty.' 'Liberty', he concluded, 'requires new definitions.' It consists in being compelled, if necessary, to do what is right. The most basic of all 'rights of man', there-fore was 'the right of the ignorant man to be guided by the wiser, to be, gently or forcibly, held in the true course by him'. This was the right 'wherein all other rights are enjoyed'.[44]

Carlyle firmly believed in the necessity of authority and of élites. No society could exist without two vital elements, an aristocracy and a priesthood, or a governing class and a teaching class. He developed this line of thought in his essay on Chartism. Needless to say, Carlyle had little liking for the Chartist programme itself, but he sympathized with the movement as an 'inarticulate uproar' from the dumb masses whose one need was to be led. Like the French Revolution, Chartism was a reaction to the ruling classes' neglect of their duty. The whole Chartist episode demonstrated to Carlyle that 'the Working Classes cannot any longer go on without government; without being *actually* guided and governed; England cannot subsist in peace till, by some means of other, some guidance and government for them is found'.[45]

In spite of his *Edinburgh Review* connections, Carlyle's hostility to polit-ical economy was almost unbounded. He thought the Enlightenment Scots 'totally destitute, to all appearances, of any patriotic affection, nay, of any human affection whatever'; and the works of that great popularizer of political economy, Harriet Martineau, were 'the acme of the Laissez-Faire system, a crisis which the sooner brings the cure'. Work was a pivotal concept in his thought. Whereas Bentham and the classical economists saw work as an evil that most people had to undergo for the sake of avoiding the greater evil of starvation, Carlyle foreshadowed Marx in thinking it crucial to personal identity, to what it is to be human. 'Properly speaking', he wrote, 'all true Work is religion'. 'All true Work is sacred', he reiterates; 'in all true Work, were it but true hand-labour, there is something of divineness.'

Carlyle liked to play the role of Cassandra, and yet his was a powerful voice in Victorian society. A number of leading political thinkers bore his imprint, the most notable being T. H. Green. But he founded no school, and the reason was perhaps that his political contacts were too eclectic and the political significance of his work too diffuse. Much as he believed authority to be indispensable to social order, Carlyle cannot be classed unproblematically as a theorist of conservatism. His article on Chartism was offered in turn to the Radical *Westminster Review* and the Tory *Quarterly Review*; and both turned it down. Carlyle was not surprised: 'Such an article, equally astonishing to Girondins, Radicals, do-nothing Aristocrats, Conservatives, and unbelieving dilettante Whigs, can hope for no harbour in any Review.' Romantic Tories of the Young England school might have sympathized with the neo-feudal vision he outlined in *Past and Present*; but he was enough of a Saint-Simonian to sense that a new aristocracy of industrialists might play this role as well as an old feudal aristocracy. On the other hand he was entirely out of sympathy with the belief that history was moving inexorably towards democracy or equality; for 'democracy is, by the nature of it, a self-cancelling business; and gives in the long-run a net result of *zero*'.[46] Like *laissez-faire*, it spelt the demise of government.

John Stuart Mill: Political Economy, History and Social Science

John Stuart Mill must inevitably figure pivotally in any history of Victorian political thought. The reason why this must be so may not be apparent to students acquainted with him chiefly through *On Liberty*, for in that text he sets himself up as a Cassandra, denouncing his age and apparently defending individuality and indeed eccentricity against social authority. But in fact he was central to the Victorian quest for a source of authority in political and social affairs. As a young man he was acutely conscious of living in an age of doctrinal conflict, and he shared Comte's conviction that a new doctrine was the only credible foundation for consensus. This perspective on Mill is vital for understanding his relationship with his contemporaries and the project he was engaged on in his two largest works, *A System of Logic* (1843) and the *Principles of Political Economy* (1848).

The utilitarian system in which Mill was brought up by his father faced challenges from three main directions in the 1820s and 1830s. Romantic poets and social critics such as Coleridge, Southey and Carlyle denied the very possibility of a scientific understanding of moral and social phenomena: the project itself entailed the reduction of man to a machine. Many Whigs dissented not from the project of a science of society, but from the particular form that science took in the utilitarian system. So Macaulay thought that a science of society might be possible – indeed,

a noble enterprise – but held that it must be based on the empirical model
of chemistry rather than the deductive model of geometry. And Saint-
Simonians and Comteans enthused about the potential of a positive
science of society to provide the basis for social reorganization, but
deplored the Ricardians' pretended science of political economy, which
must necessarily fail because social phenomena formed an interlocking
system, and it was impossible to divorce one kind of social phenomenon
from the rest and study it in isolation.

Mill absorbed these three lines of criticism of the utilitarian system,
and in response set out to refine it to bolster its ability to command
authority without blunting its cutting edge. There is an influential view
that these critiques turned Mill into a self-conscious eclectic whose most
notable gift was the ability to see both sides of an argument and to produce a synthesis of opposites. But the alternative view is that these critics
failed to dislodge Mill from his fundamental commitment to political
radicalism and to philosophical empiricism. A close analysis of Mill's
methodological writings surely confirms this second view. The chapter
in Book VI of the *Logic* which Mill devotes to the discussion of the 'chemical, or experimental, method in the social science' should be read as an
outright denunciation of Macaulay. For though the historian and Edinburgh reviewer is not mentioned by name, there can be little doubt who
is intended by the reference to 'persons with greater pretensions to
instruction . . . who, having heard that Bacon taught mankind to follow
experience, and to ground their conclusions on facts instead of metaphysical dogmas – think that, by treating political facts in as directly
experimental a method as chemical facts, they are showing themselves
true Baconians, and proving their adversaries to be mere syllogizers and
schoolmen'.[47] One of Macaulay's chief allegations against the elder Mill
was that he had ignored Baconian principles and had approached the
science of government as 'an Aristotelian of the fifteenth century, born
out of due season'.

It is quite true that in the *Logic* Mill rejected his father's project of constructing a deductive social science on the pattern of geometry. But this
was scarcely a concession to Macaulay at all. Mill conceived of a science of
politics – indeed any social science – by means of the analogy of the concept of the composition of forces. Political and social phenomena were to
be assimilated to *mechanical* phenomena rather than to *chemical* phenomena. A science must be deductive rather than experimental if, in the
province with which it deals, the effects of causes when conjoined are the
sums of the effects that the same causes produce when separate.[48] But

Macaulay's whole argument could be read as the claim that according to this very principle politics should be an experimental science. For, in criticizing the elder Mill for seeking to deduce the 'science of government' from the principles of human nature, Macaulay posed the following dilemma. Is the experience from which James Mill deduces the principles of human nature experience of man in politics or experience of pre-political man?

If it includes experience of the manner in which men act when intrusted with the powers of government, then those principles of human nature from which the science of government is to be deduced, can only be known after going through that inductive process by which we propose to arrive at the science of government. Our knowledge of human nature, instead of being prior in order to our knowledge of the science of government, will be posterior to it.

Macaulay thought this a devastating criticism, but the younger Mill was apparently unimpressed, for he was quite clear that 'men are not, when brought together, converted into another kind of substance, with different properties. . . . Human beings in society have no properties but those which are derived from, and may be resolved into, the laws of the nature of individual man'.[49]

To Comte, Mill had a specific debt: from him he learnt how the historical method – the 'inverse deductive' method, Mill called it – might get him out of his methodological difficulties. Mill is sometimes portrayed as an abstract and unhistorical thinker, but if we consider his work as a whole this is a highly misleading conclusion. He enthusiastically embraced the historical-mindedness of the age. He wrote perceptively and admiringly about Guizot, Michelet and other writers of the French historical school, and indeed chided his English contemporaries for their superficial understanding of history and their neglect of its philosophy. Mill fully accepted the doctrine, taught by German romantics and French Saint-Simonians alike, that ideas and institutions had to be understood in their time and place; and it was this historicism that persuaded him that the methods of political economy were not directly applicable to social science as a whole. 'A philosophy of law and institutions, not founded on a philosophy of national character, is an absurdity.'[50] A recurrent and fascinating theme in Mill's writings is his attempt to reconcile his acceptance of the truth in historicism with his ongoing quest for a reforming science of society.

It is sometimes argued that there was no real contradiction here. Mill did not learn the philosophy of history from Coleridge or from Saint-Simon, but from his father, whose *History of India* made him one of the foremost historians of the age. But this is surely a mistake. James Mill's historical writings belonged to the Enlightenment genre of philosophic history: like Condorcet he saw history in terms of the gradual stripping away of ignorance, superstition and other obstacles to progress. So the *History of India* was conceived as a contest between light and darkness. Absent were the romantics' particularism – their sense of institutions as the expression of the spirit of the age or of the national character – and the Saint-Simonians' conception of society as a *system*. These were understandings of history that J. S. Mill encountered in thinkers such as Coleridge and Comte, both of whom stood outside the utilitarian system.

What perturbed Mill about historicism was that it threatened to blunt the reformist or even radical edge that was essential to his conception of social science. His worry was that an historicist social science would be quietistic: it would tend to show that what is, has to be. This was why he rejected Macaulay's proposed 'chemical' method for social science: because Macaulay repudiated the prospect of connecting a science of government with principles of human nature, he implicitly accepted (so Mill thought) that that science could not serve as the foundation for a radical critique of existing institutions. The 'inverse deductive' method was useful to Mill because on the one hand it confirmed the irrevocably historicist character of the social sciences, while on the other hand it allowed him to avert the danger of quietism because the inductive generalizations from history could attain scientific (and hence authoritative) status only if they could in principle be deduced from known laws of mind.

Here we get close to understanding why Mill's relationship with his contemporaries hovered between that of the authoritative and fair-minded teacher and that of the dangerous partisan. He endorsed the Benthamites' aim of constructing a social science that would serve as the foundation for the fundamental recasting of the institutions of society. But he realized that the Benthamite system was too narrow in its foundations to command the broad assent it would need if it were to serve as the basis for the kind of institutional reform envisaged. He therefore set himself the objective of constructing a more adequate methodological foundation for reformist social science, and he saw that in order to do this he would have to be able to demonstrate a systematic and rationally cognizable relationship between the laws of human nature in the abstract and the particular forms it takes at particular times and in particular places. This was the point of a favourite but famously unrealized project of Mill's, his science of ethology, or the science 'which determines the kind of character produced in conformity to those general laws [of psychology] by any set of circumstances, physical or moral'.

When we come to examine Mill's best-known work, *On Liberty*, we shall see just how far it was shaped by this same preoccupation with education and the formation of character. It was vital to his project as a liberal and a social scientist to be able to show that character was both *made* and *self*-made. But first we need to examine how these essentially moral concerns infused Victorian individualism more generally.

Individualism and Beyond

Liberals of Mill's generation broadly shared their predecessors' presumption against the growth of state power, but their reasons for making this presumption were subtly different. The change betokened a new kind of liberalism which was to be built upon by T. H. Green and his generation, much as they thought they were reacting against it. Bentham and James Mill had taken it as axiomatic that state compulsion was an infringement of liberty, and that it would have to be justified on other grounds such as security or justice. They also held that individuals should in general be assumed to be the best judge of their own interest, from which they inferred that in general the free operation of the market would be most likely to yield 'the greatest happiness of the greatest number'. They thought of political institutions as contrivances for realizing the wants and preferences of individuals. Mid-Victorian liberals departed from this approach because even when they assented to utilitarianism, as J. S. Mill did, their cast of thought was altogether too developmentalist to take 'interests' or 'wants' as static givens whose satisfaction it would be the aim of public policy to facilitate. Long before Darwin wrote, a profound consciousness of time had already begun to transform the Victorian mental landscape, as both German historical scholarship and the geological sciences suggested that phenomena should be understood dynamically, as the product of a long accumulation of almost imperceptible but incremental changes. Mill, for example, came to believe that social institutions had to be considered in the light of a philosophy of history. But this notion had clear and far-reaching implications for public policy. For the satisfaction of the actual wants of the moment might hinder the individual's realization of his full potential, and he might become the creature of those wants rather than their master. This point can best be understood if we examine the discourse of 'character', with whose pervasive influence on Victorian social, political and moral thought we have been made familiar through the work of Stefan Collini.

The first point to stress about the concept of character is that it is difficult to reconcile with the hedonism which is often thought to have permeated the outlook of the early Victorians under the influence of utilitarians. As a type of ethical doctrine hedonism is by its nature both static and empirical: it takes the satisfaction of *actual wants*, whatever they may be, to be the criterion of moral conduct and public policy. Wants are taken as given. The practical force of the idea of character was to replace this essentially static perspective with a dynamic and educative one. Wants came to be seen as the creatures of character, and character was formed in part by habit; so that the present satisfaction of 'lower' wants might hinder the unfolding of 'higher' wants in the future. In short, the significance of the concept of character was that it marked a clear recognition that there was more to selfhood than empirical, day-to-day wants. Those empirical wants should be appraised very differently according to whether they were merely arbitrary desires, or the product of a settled and rational character which was capable of subduing and ordering wants as necessary in order to dominate rather than be buffeted by circumstances.

But what were the implications of the idea of character for the debate over the limits of government intervention? They were complex, and by no means unilinear. On the one hand there was a deep-seated and tenacious conviction that self-reliance alone fostered a vigorous and manly character, and that a pattern of reliance on others, whether charitable institutions or the state, sapped any remaining resources of independence. 'The mental and the moral, like the muscular, powers are improved only by being used', wrote Mill in *On Liberty*.[51] Anti-statists such as Samuel Smiles and Herbert Spencer were among the most prominent exponents of the language of character.

Nevertheless, the language of character had an important implication which tended to undermine the caricature of rugged and self-reliant individualism. For it insistently highlighted the importance of social circumstances for the promotion of moral qualities, and subtly insinuated into the Victorian consciousness the idea that public agencies had a role to play in creating the sort of environment in which desirable moral qualities might flourish. 'Social' reforms often aimed not so much at structural as at moral reform, the creation of circumstances in which qualities such as sobriety, thrift and sexual modesty could develop. The revision of liberalism in a more 'collectivist' direction by T. H. Green and his successors effectively systematized this tendency; drawing upon themes that were already present in Mill's thought, but seeking to give them a more adequate philosophical foundation.

It is sometimes argued that the language of character was more characteristic of the late Victorian period, and that earlier invocations of it – in the works of Mill and Carlyle, for instance – should be read as anticipations of the social theory of a later generation. This argument is linked to an emphasis on the hegemony of utilitarianism and hedonism over early Victorian social thought.[52] It underpins an influential narrative which tends to exaggerate the gulf between early- and late-Victorian outlooks. The classic popular exposition of the idea of character was Samuel Smiles's *Character*, published in 1871. But Smiles was an early Victorian, a fact often obscured by his longevity: he was born just six years after Mill and reached adulthood before Victoria ascended the throne. His best-known work, *Self-Help*, was published in 1859, the year Mill published *On Liberty*; and it revolved around the concept of character just as much as did the work entitled *Character*. Its full title, indeed, was *Self-Help: with Illustrations of Character and Conduct*; and its final chapter was headed 'Character – The True Gentleman'. The ascendancy of the language of character may be dated, then, from the middle of the century.

Hedonism, or the doctrine that the common good is produced spontaneously by individuals' pursuit of their own happiness, was almost as remote from the outlook of the secular liberal defenders of *laissez-faire* as from that of the Christian political economists. It is helpful to consider Smiles and his works in this context, not because he was either an original or a systematic thinker, but because he has a certain claim to representative status. He was one of the great myth-makers of Victorian Britain, 'the authorized and pious chronicler of the men who founded the industrial greatness of England'.[53] The very titles of his works – *Character*, *Thrift* and *Duty* – serve to convey something of the scent of Victorian values. *Self-Help*, in particular, was an enormous publishing success: it sold twenty thousand copies within a year, fifty-five thousand within five years, and over a quarter of a million by the time its author died in 1905.[54] He is particularly interesting for our purposes given that Benthamism was an undoubted influence on his thinking, though it was an influence tempered by that of the American unitarians Emerson and Channing.

Smiles apparently sympathized with Harriet Martineau's professed belief that society was no more than an aggregate of individuals. Men, he wrote, 'must be dealt with as units; for it is only by the elevation of individuals that the elevation of the masses can be effectively secured'.[55] The action of the state, he thought, was as nothing beside the moral qualities of the individuals composing it, and 'all experience serves to prove that the worth and strength of a State depend far less upon the form of its institutions than upon the character of its men. For the nation is only the aggregate of individual conditions, and civilization itself is but a question of personal improvement.'[56] But Smiles intended these not as ontological truths but as normative propositions. And when read carefully his works turn out to be more complex than they seem when summarized in a thumbnail sketch. Two points need to be made here: the first about the relationship between character and circumstances, and the second about Smiles's concept of liberty.

As Stefan Collini has shown, Victorian moralists posited a dialectical relationship between character and circumstances. Strength of character manifested itself primarily in the mastery of circumstances, but character itself was, to a greater or lesser extent, the product of circumstances. This point should serve to qualify the individualism of the early Victorians. 'Man is not the creature, so much as the creator of circumstance', wrote Smiles;[57] but in practice he tempered this claim, for he recognized that one part of the process of character-formation was care to expose oneself to the right sort of influences. One's character is shaped by those one associates with – a claim that is deeply unindividualistic in its implications. 'Moral health', Smiles wrote, depends upon 'the moral atmosphere that is breathed', so that 'it is advisable...for young men to seek the fellowship of the good, and always to aim at a higher standard than themselves'.[58] Smiles was well aware of what this implied. 'No individual in the universe stands alone; he is a component part of a system of mutual dependencies; and by his several acts, he either increases or diminishes the sum of human good now and for ever.'[59] A statement like this, imbued with a sense of the interdependence of the individual and society, would later become something of a commonplace in late-Victorian moral and social discourse; and it is illuminating to find it articulated by a writer such as Smiles. What it brings home is that the 'individualism' of the early Victorians was formulated in opposition to the state; in the case of lower middle-class radicals such as Smiles, in opposition to a state which was perceived as controlled not by public opinion but by sectional interests. It did not imply a lack of a sense of the reality of 'society'. Early- and

mid-Victorian individualism certainly entailed a marked preference for
self-reliance over state action; but this preference was rooted in a developmental rather than a static ethical outlook. Self-reliance was good
because it had a bracing effect on character: it forced individuals to exercise their higher qualities, and by exercising to develop them. But individualism was not on the whole based on an atomistic conception of
society, nor on a merely empirical conception of the self.

This understanding of the relationship between character and circumstances had consequences for Smiles's concept of liberty. We might expect
to find in Smiles a forthright statement of the idea of negative liberty – a
defence of the individual's right to pursue the satisfaction of his or her
wants, whatever those wants may be, and constrained only by a recognition of the equivalent rights of other individuals. But in practice this
doctrine, given classical expression by Bentham, was difficult to reconcile with the moral hegemony of the concept of character, associated as it
was (not least in Smiles) with an emphasis on the importance of habit. For
the pursuit of 'lower' wants (self-gratification as opposed to thrift, for
instance) – if repeated – would have permanently corrosive consequences
for the moral character. That was the significance of the language of
'slavery' to the desires, which is a recurrent feature of the language of
positive liberty – of the belief that liberty consists in the power to pursue the
goals of self-culture and self-improvement. Smiles, who had once been
active in political radicalism in Leeds, had by the 1840s become disillusioned with political life; and in *Self-Help* he articulated his political indifference. 'The greatest slave', he now insisted, 'is not he who is ruled by a
despot, great though that evil be, but he who is in thrall of his own moral
ignorance, selfishness, and vice'. 'Individual character', not a particular
set of political institutions, was the only sure foundation of liberty.[60]

Clearly this insight into Smiles's concept of liberty entails a rethinking
of the conventional narrative of Victorian political thought, which holds
that a 'negative' concept of liberty, defined as *freedom from* external
impediments, held sway up to the 1870s or 1880s. At that point the
impact of philosophical idealism cleared the way for a more adequate
and 'positive' concept, which redefined liberty in substantive terms as
the totality of conditions necessary for human beings to realize their
potential. This new concept of liberty made possible a more constructive
understanding of the ability of state action to enhance liberty by providing or guaranteeing those conditions.

This is a misleading account because it conflates two issues that are
analytically distinct. On the one hand there is the philosophical question

of whether liberty is better understood in formal or in substantive terms; on the other hand there is the more empirical question of whether liberty is likely to be constrained or enhanced by the action of the state. Clearly, a negative libertarian – a follower of Hobbes or Bentham, perhaps – would necessarily believe state action to be by its very nature restrictive of liberty, and to that extent a bad thing, though the loss of liberty might well be outweighed by other goods, such as greater equality or greater security. But it does not follow that a positive libertarian, who ties liberty to man's ability to determine himself, will necessarily uphold extensive state action as a means of enhancing liberty. I want to suggest that Smiles was by no means unusual among liberals of his generation in understanding freedom in 'positive' terms, as the potential for self-realization; but that he was also quite typical of his age in thinking state action bad because it encouraged a condition of dependency.

To substantiate this argument we need to return to Mill, as the author of the most famous discussion of the concept of liberty in the whole of the nineteenth century.

Mill's *On Liberty* is the one Victorian text which now enjoys undisputed canonical status in political theory; but conventional readings of it are misleading. It is often taken as an archetypal exposition of the philosophy of Victorian liberalism, yet Mill considered it a biting critique of the pieties and commonplaces of the age, and critics noted with dismay his 'contempt for the common ways of Englishmen'. Likewise, his essay is often read as the *locus classicus* of a negative liberalism which conceived liberty as the individual's right to follow his or her own will, untrammelled by interference from the state or from an intrusive public opinion. This reading too is misconceived. Mill certainly sought to defend individual freedom against pressures for conformity from Middle England. But it would be quite untrue to assert that his liberalism was indifferent as between different conceptions of the good life. Still less did he attach priority to the satisfaction of the actual wants of the present generation, irrespective of what those wants might be. In fact the essay belongs squarely within that strand of Victorian moral discourse which gave priority to 'character'. Mill's aim was above all to demonstrate the superiority of the 'self-determined' character over the character that is the mere product of circumstance, and the superiority of the 'active and energetic' type of character over the 'inert and torpid' type which he associated with the Christian ethic of submissiveness and resignation. His conception of liberty rested on a determinate and distinctive conception of the self.

The distinctive quality of the positive concept of liberty is that it suggests that freedom entails not so much the absence of external constraints as the empowerment to do 'what I am called on to do'. In other words, unlike the negative concept it cannot aspire to value-neutrality, but entails a more or less determinate conception of what it means to be 'fully' human. In this sense, I want to argue, Mill's concept of liberty was thoroughly positive. For in *On Liberty* he expounded a particular conception of the good life – of what it means to be human – and his argument was infused with the language of 'positive' liberty. In his chapter entitled 'Of Individuality, as one of the elements of well-being', he identifies certain desires, certain ways of life as distinctively human, and contrasts them with custom-bound ways of life which, as Mill understood them, did not exercise the distinctively human faculties at all. These latter ways of life were, Mill thought, appropriate either to other species (apes, sheep) or to machines (the steam-engine is mentioned), but not to human beings. He writes of individuals enslaved to their desires, their mind 'bowed to the yoke' of custom, and this is the characteristic language in which the concept of positive liberty is expounded.[61] Furthermore, Mill's concept of the self was profoundly developmental in its assumptions. A person who does not 'choose his plan of life . . . for himself' but merely follows the dictates of social convention fails to exercise 'the human faculties of perception, judgement, discriminative feeling, mental activity, and even moral preference'; and because of this failure, this person loses his opportunity of realizing his full potential as a progressive being. This notion that the higher, more distinctively human, qualities stagnate and deteriorate when not used was characteristic of a great deal of mid-Victorian moral discourse. It fed on a pervasive assumption that anything that does not progress is doomed to decline.

Yet Mill has commonly been viewed as the quintessential 'negative' liberal, and the reason is that in *On Liberty* he makes out a strong case for the instrumental value of negative liberty for the achievement of the goals of the positive libertarian. The absence of constraint is an indispensable condition for the realization of our full potential as human beings. If people are forced, by law or public opinion, to adopt or adhere to a particular set of values or a particular style of life, then they will not learn the distinctively human capacity to choose. Freedom, in Mill's thought, derives its value from a concept of the good life; but it is the nature of that concept of the good life – hinging as it does on the capacity to think out one's opinions and style of life rationally for oneself – that it cannot be imposed on people, but can be learned only through the exercise of

liberty. For Mill, therefore, there was no sharp distinction between negative and positive concepts of liberty: for him, unlike for Rousseau, it
could make no sense to speak of being 'forced to be free'.

On Liberty, then, was anything but a manifesto for hedonism. Whereas
earlier Benthamites had believed that social improvement was to be
accomplished through the enlightenment of 'selfish feelings', Mill
increasingly followed Comte in believing that progress would spring
from the supersession of hedonism by altruism. He attached a great deal
of importance to the formation of a 'religion of humanity'; a point that is
obscured by his vigorous critique of Comte's particular version of that
religion. For Mill this religion would be no pale substitute for Christianity, but an improvement upon it, because it would rest on a selfless devotion to the general good, and not (like Christianity) on a mere fear of
future punishment.[62] In Utilitarianism he wrote of the need for social
institutions to 'place the happiness, or . . . the interest, of every individual,
as nearly as possible in harmony with the interest of the whole', and for
education and the power of opinion to be so deployed 'as to establish in
the mind of every individual an indissoluble association between his own
happiness and the good of the whole'. Classical liberalism had travelled
a long way from Adam Smith's invisible hand. Far from supposing that
individuals' pursuit of their own happiness would, through the operation of the market, be conducive to the interests of others, Mill now held
that social progress demanded that individuals should be so educated as
to want only those things which were constitutive of the general good.
This point of view was voiced most eloquently in his Autobiography, where
he maintained that 'the deep rooted selfishness which forms the general
character of the existing state of society, is so deeply rooted, only because
the whole course of existing institutions tends to foster it'. It was Mill's
conviction that 'education, habit, and the cultivation of the sentiments
will make a common man dig or weave for his country, as readily as fight
for his country'. Social institutions must be so designed as to promote
'interest in the common good'.[63]

This account of On Liberty might appear paradoxical, given Mill's famous distinction between 'self-regarding' and 'other-regarding' actions.
But in fact commentators such as the German philosopher Jürgen Hab-
ermas have been misled by Mill's revulsion at the intrusive way in which
Victorian public opinion invaded the sphere of 'self-regarding' actions,
and have thus overlooked the importance he assigned to 'publicity', or
to the role of public opinion in inducing the individual citizen to
consider questions from the point of view of the social whole. As far as

'other-regarding' actions were concerned, Mill not only permitted but encouraged public opinion to subject the behaviour of individuals to inspection. Those who used the vote frivolously or selfishly – so he argued in *Considerations on Representative Government* (1861) – should be required to answer for their conduct. This was why Mill abandoned his early support for the secret ballot in favour of the retention of open voting.

The other point to underline about *On Liberty* is that, like practically all Mill's writings on political and social questions, it is couched in explicitly *developmental* terms. As he put it in his *Autobiography*, Mill assumed that questions of social and political institutions should be determined chiefly 'by the consideration, what great improvement in life and culture stands next in order for the people concerned, as the condition of their further progress, and what institutions are most likely to promote that'. Mill had learnt from the Coleridgeans, from Maurice, Carlyle and others, that 'time, place, and circumstance' were of critical importance in politics.[64] But this teaching never made him quiescent in his attitude to social institutions and practices. He never accepted that what is, has to be. Instead, awareness of the importance of time, place and circumstance made him first and foremost a moral rather than a mechanical reformer. The whole cast of his mature mind led him to consider political questions from an educative point of view. Centralized institutions might, in the short term, be more productive of happiness than institutions that fed on self-help and voluntary association. But the former might destroy the seeds of moral improvement, whereas the latter tend to promote them. This was an argument Mill propounded both in *On Liberty* and in *Considerations on Representative Government*. In the final chapter of the former work he briefly discussed institutions such as jury trials and democratic local government, which might be thought deficient from the point of view of mechanical efficiency, but which could better be considered as 'questions of development'. In other words they formed part of 'national education; as being, in truth, the peculiar training of a citizen, the practical part of the political education of a free people, taking them out of the narrow circle of personal and family selfishness, and accustoming them to the comprehension of joint interests, the management of joint concerns – habituating them to act from public or semi-public motives, and guide their conduct by aims which unite instead of isolating them from one another'.[65] Mill developed this argument at greater length in *Representative Government*, especially in the chapter headed 'The criterion of a good form of government.' There he contended that the most important cause of good or bad government lay in 'the qualities of the human beings composing the society over which the government is exercised'. From this he inferred that the first question to ask of any set of political institutions was 'how far they tend to foster in the members of the community the various desirable qualities, moral and intellectual'.[66] The besetting weakness of 'Oriental despotism' was its tendency to stunt the growth of the moral and mental qualities of the people, and hence to stifle their potential for future development.[67]

In *On Liberty* Mill was not primarily concerned with questions of *laissez-faire* and state intervention. That was an issue he tackled chiefly in his most authoritative work, the *Principles of Political Economy* (1848), and especially in Book V, where he discussed the 'limits to the province of government'. His arguments here can be read as a Victorian translation of Adam Smith's encounter with the civic tradition. Smith, as we have seen, explored ways in which government action might help encourage the kind of public spirit – undermined by the advancement of the division of labour – which could prevent government being suborned by sectional interests. Mill, like many other Victorians who had read their Tocqueville, was less inclined to see the progress of civil society as innately corrosive of civic virtue, and in a very characteristic line of argument he suggested that there should be a presumption against state action because its tendency was to supplant spontaneous initiatives at the level of civil society and hence to render the public passive and helpless. 'A people among whom there is no habit of spontaneous action for a collective interest – who look habitually to their government to command or prompt them in all matters of joint concern – who expect to have everything done for them, except what can be made an affair of mere habit and routine – have their faculties only half developed; their education is defective in one of its most important branches.'[68]

A situation in which the state was seen as the chief agent of social progress, and in which a wide gulf opened up between the intelligence of a bureaucratic elite and that of the people at large, was dangerous to public liberty. 'The only security against political slavery is the check maintained over governors by the diffusion of intelligence, activity, and public spirit among the governed.' It was not just 'self-regarding' matters that should be left to private individuals themselves; in addition it was highly desirable that, where possible, matters of collective interest should be dealt with by 'voluntary cooperation' rather than by state action. And the reason was stated in unmistakably Tocquevillian terms: 'this discussion and management of collective interests is the great school of that public spirit, and the great source of that intelligence of public affairs, which are always regarded as the distinctive character of the public of free countries'. In short, 'a democratic constitution, not supported by democratic institutions in detail, but confined to the central government, not only is not political freedom, but often creates a spirit precisely the reverse, carrying down to the lowest grade in society the desire and ambition of political domination'.[69]

Compulsory elementary education at the public expense was, for Mill as for Smith, an important exception to the principle of *laissez-faire*. Why? Because whereas most forms of state action tend to weaken desirable qualities of civic virtue and public spirit, education ought to have the opposite effect. 'Instruction, when it is really such, does not enervate, but strengthens as well as enlarges the active faculties: in whatever manner acquired, its effect on the mind is favourable to the spirit of independence: and when, unless and gratuitously, it would not be had at all, help in this form has the opposite tendency to that which in so many other cases makes it objectionable; it is help towards doing without help.' In short, Mill's general opposition to the extension of state action was founded on a presumption that it would militate against individuals' realization of their highest potential. But where it could be demonstrated that state action would supplement rather than supplant free individuals, Mill looked on it with favour.

If Victorian thinking does not easily fit our familiar stereotypes of 'classical liberalism', this may be because those stereotypes have paid insufficient attention to the ambiguities of liberalism as a doctrine of government. For, on the one hand, liberalism may be defined as that doctrine which, taking for granted that society consists of autonomous individuals, set out to protect those individuals from the encroachments of society and the state. But on the other hand liberalism may equally be viewed as a doctrine which, far from taking a society of autonomous individuals for granted, instead set out to bring such a society into being. In this sense it did not rest on neutrality as between different conceptions of the good life, but on a distinct preference for one particular conception.[70]

Continuity and Change in Victorian Political Thought

The idea that there was a rupture in Victorian social and political thought about the 1860s and 1870s has long been widely accepted, although a number of different accounts are offered as to why things changed. One account, first advanced by Leslie Stephen, emphasizes the impact of the Darwinian revolution, which is said to have undermined the essentially static model of man deployed by the utilitarians. A second account, favoured by the Oxford idealists, identifies a philosophical revolution associated with the English discovery of Hegel as the crucial factor which swept away the foundations of the old, negative liberalism and cleared the way for a fuller appreciation of the positive role of the state in removing the obstacles to liberty. A third account focuses on internal developments within political economy: the collapse of the classical paradigm in the 1860s meant that economics was no longer able to command an authoritative standing in social thought.

All three accounts are one-sided and vulnerable to criticism. The 'Darwinian' interpretation has been difficult to swallow ever since John Burrow, writing in the 1960s, showed just how pervasive evolutionary ideas were in Victorian social thought in the decades *before* Darwin wrote. The philosophical version overlooks the degree to which 'old' liberals – whether theorists such as Mill or popularizers such as Smiles – were open to 'positive' concepts of liberty. It also neglects an important strand within early Victorian political thought – best represented, perhaps, by Thomas Arnold – which stressed the constructive role of the state in furnishing the conditions for the good life. Meanwhile the third account assumes that the hegemony enjoyed by political economy from the 1820s to the 1860s rested essentially upon the internal coherence of the classical model. The implication of Boyd Hilton's work is surely that the appeal of political economy owed much more to its ability to dovetail with the deeply rooted moral assumptions of the age. The market, freed from paternalistic interference by government or parish officers, would reward thrift and prudence and punish improvidence and idleness. The beneficence of this mechanism was common ground to secular utilitarians and to those such as Thomas Chalmers who wished to give it a theological significance.

Hilton takes 1865 as the end-point of his study of the 'age of atonement', but the implication of his account is that the most important shift in Victorian social thought took place somewhat earlier, being a product of the age of prosperity of the 1850s. A new incarnational theology imparted a gentler tone to the moral and social thought of the mid-Victorian period. It was also connected with a growing sense that the divine was revealed in and through human history. Theologically the emphasis was now incarnational; and politically there was a revaluation of social relations and human institutions, which were no longer scorned as the products of a fallen world, but interpreted in quasi-sacramental terms as signs and channels of the divine grace. Thus while Christian social thought in the first decades of the nineteenth century may have been evangelical and individualistic in its emphasis, by the middle of the Victorian period the emphasis had been radically shifted by such thinkers as F. D. Maurice.

2

THE STATE OF THE NATION: HISTORY, CULTURE AND DEMOCRACY

The utilitarians' and political economists' focus on interest as the bond of society never extinguished an equally powerful Victorian concern with questions of identity. These were universal questions for nineteenth-century European states, whether or not they underwent territorial upheaval, as Germany and Italy did. Who counted as a citizen, as a full member of the political nation? The question of nationality underlay the debates on the extension of the franchise that extended throughout the Victorian period, but it also pervaded many other recurrent political issues of the period, in particular those concerned with religion, education and empire.

On the whole the utilitarian tradition furnished few intellectual resources with which to tackle questions of nationhood and identity. Some classical economists thought of national boundaries as mere frictions interfering with the free play of the market. Instead, Victorian discussions of these themes were nourished by religion, history and the classics. In particular, I want to highlight two important intellectual traditions which sustained reflection upon nationhood. The more familiar was constitutional history, and especially the historiographical tradition known as 'Whig' history. That tradition will be examined presently. But first we need to consider a more neglected tradition in which theology rather than secular historiography was the main driving force. We have already seen Coleridge outlining the important function of nationality as a social bond; and the group of writers who developed this theme furthest were Coleridge's intellectual descendants, the Liberal Anglican or

Broad Church school. This tradition can be traced from Thomas Arnold and F. D. Maurice to its late representatives in an age of crisis of faith, such men as Matthew Arnold and J. R. Seeley. Influenced by the rediscovery of the work of the Neapolitan philosopher of the early Enlightenment, Giambattista Vico, these thinkers reflected in depth about the relationship between particular communities and universal values, between national history and world history, and their work as a whole constituted a major rehabilitation of social institutions as sacramental pointers to universal values. Whereas utilitarians and classical economists dealt with individual interest and the general good, the Liberal Anglican tradition focused on those institutions and communities that mediated between them.

Liberal Anglicanism

The Liberal Anglican intellectual stance was important in part because it echoed two of the most tenacious concerns of nineteenth-century political thought in continental Europe: the exploration of national identity and the quest for consensus and order in the post-revolutionary world. Indeed, if an English parallel is sought for the characteristic concerns of continental European political thought in the nineteenth century – the concerns of Fichte and Michelet and Mazzini, of Renan and Treitschke – it is most likely to be found among the Liberal Anglicans who, descended from Coleridge and Thomas Arnold, were preoccupied with ideas of nationality, culture and the organic state. Whereas Whigs and utilitarians shared a preoccupation with interest, these thinkers saw will as the foundation of the state. Long before T. H. Green wrote, the concept of a moralized state had an important place in the Liberal Anglican tradition, deeply influenced as it was by the revival of interest in ancient Greek thought. Thomas Arnold, perhaps the most significant writer in this tradition, defended 'the moral theory of a state', which he considered 'the foundation of political truth'.[1] The Liberal Anglicans have not featured prominently in most accounts of Victorian political and social thought, but they were culturally central, not least because of their domination of the ancient universities from the 1840s. The purpose of the following section is to rectify the neglect of this tradition by historians of Victorian political thought.

Thomas Arnold

The philosophical genius of the Liberal Anglican tradition was Coleridge, and he has by no means been neglected by historians of political thought, although his essentially unclassifiable genius is distorted by the reading of him as a simple theoretician of conservatism. It was only after his death that Coleridge was appropriated by the Conservatives; and the fact that his American disciples called themselves Whigs should alert us to the adaptability of his political outlook. But if Coleridge was the philosopher of Liberal Anglicanism, it was Thomas Arnold who did more than anyone to form it into a coherent doctrine and to propagate it. Arnold is best known to historians as an educational reformer, the man who as Headmaster of Rugby School 'changed the face of education all through the public schools of England'; and secondly as a churchman, a leader of the Oxford branch of Liberal Anglicanism. His significance as a political thinker has by comparison been neglected; but improperly so, for neither his educational nor his ecclesiastical activities can be fully understood except as aspects of a broader commitment to national reform; and that in turn cannot be understood except in the light of his vision of the ethical state. He deserves an important place in any study of Victorian political thought, not least because his influence was so far-reaching. It was not just the Broad Churchmen who were touched by his ideas, but Liberal Nationalist historians such as the Gladstonian E. A. Freeman and the Imperialist J. R. Seeley; positivists such as the Rugbeian Richard Congreve; and Christian Socialists such as F. D. Maurice.

Arnold was perhaps the foremost early Victorian exponent of the doctrine of the ethical state.[2] He defended his 'moral theory of the objects of a state' against Macaulay's pronouncement that 'the object of political society is the preservation of body and goods'.[3] Macaulay had restated that eighteenth-century doctrine in opposition to Gladstone's extravagant assertion of the idea of the national church as the conscience of the state; but Arnold contended that Macaulay had confused the issue by supposing the nub of the moral theory to be that the state's end is the propagation of religious truth – a theory which, by tying the state to a particular church, had clearly objectionable consequences in Arnold's eyes. It was much more defensible, he argued, if reformulated to propose as the state's end the promotion of 'man's highest perfection'. In other words, Arnold insisted that spiritual and moral unity could act as a social bond, whereas the attempt to use doctrinal unity as the basis of social cohesion was necessarily chimerical. 'All societies of men, whether we call them states or churches, should make their bond to consist in a common object and a common practice, rather than in a common belief; in other words, their end should be good rather than truth. We may consent to act together, but we cannot consent to believe together.' In the early church, the original bond was a 'union of action' rather than credal uniformity; and though a closer union of belief came about, the key point was that 'it was the result of belonging to the society rather than a previous condition required for belonging to it'.[4]

This argument led Arnold to the proposition that 'no human power can presume to enquire into the degree of a man's positive belief'; but it might nevertheless require outward submission to the law of Christianity. 'If a man believes himself bound to refuse obedience to the law of Christianity, or will not pledge himself to regard it as paramount in authority to any human legislation, he cannot properly be a member of a society which conceives itself bound to regulate all its proceedings by this law, and cannot allow any of its provisions to be regarded as revocable or alterable.'[5]

Arnold's concept of the ethical state had far-reaching implications for the concept of citizenship, which, in Britain as in continental Europe, was being renegotiated in the aftermath of the French Revolution. In France and Germany the problem of military service directed the attention of political and legal theorists towards the definition of state membership. In Britain, which had no citizen-army, the vital question was religion. After all, Britain had been a confessional state in which Roman Catholics and to a lesser extent Protestant nonconformists were excluded from political rights. As the crisis of the confessional state came to a head in the late 1820s, not least in consequence of the Act of Union with Ireland of 1800, an inescapable question arose: in a Christian state with an established Church which had its own quasi-credal articles of religion, to what extent could the terms of citizenship be relaxed so as to open public office to Protestant dissenters, to Roman Catholics, to non-Trinitarian Christians, and to non-Christians, especially Jews?

This question has not been adequately treated as an issue in nineteenth-century political thought. It was in fact the central question Arnold confronted in his writings on the state. His religious latitudinarianism, it is now clear, was directed *against* those who wished to reduce the state to a society founded upon mere interest alone. Those who tied political rights to narrow religious dogma made it much harder, in Arnold's view, to draw the vital distinction between citizens and subjects:

between those who share in the moral and spiritual life of the state, and those who simply enjoy the benefits of the state's protection. For Arnold was certain that religion, which for him meant the profession of Christianity, had to be the 'bond and test of citizenship' in modern European states, playing the role that in ancient polities had been played by racial homogeneity.[6] Religion was the one bond capable of raising the state above the level of a government instituted for the low purposes of policing a society. The implication was that whereas it was quite proper for Protestant nonconformists and Roman Catholics to be received into full citizenship, the same principle could by no means be extended to (non-baptized) Jews. Proposals to admit Jews to political rights were founded on what Arnold dismissed as a 'low Jacobinical notion of citizenship, that a man acquires a right to it by the accident of his being littered inter quatuor maria, or because he pays taxes'.[7] The Jews, he told Whately, should be considered 'voluntary strangers' in Britain, having 'no claim to become citizens, but by conforming to our moral law, which is the Gospel'.[8] For the same reason, and because he considered universities to be essential national institutions, he used his membership of the Senate of the University of London to fight a lonely and unsuccessful battle against the conferment of degrees on Jews in 1838.

Arnold's stance on the question of Jewish emancipation was plainly conservative and bordered on the obscurantist. But the reason why he felt so strongly about the issue was that it brought into question whether the state had ethical or merely pragmatic objectives; and the ethical concept of the state was, by his lights, progressive. Arnold is in fact rather difficult to place politically. He was certainly no radical. He despised Jacobinism, as well as 'all that godless Utilitarianism' which he took to be the English form of Jacobinism. He was vehemently anti-Benthamite, and thought that contemporary liberals and radicals overrated both Bentham personally and political economists as a class. He was as contemptuous as his son Matthew was to be of the ethos of Manchester liberalism, that 'mere money-getting and money-saving selfishness which cries aloud for *cheap* government'. Though he opposed the Corn Laws and the growth of the national debt, he was also sceptical of political economy's claims to authority. 'A doctrine may be perfectly true as far as regards political economy, but not true as regards the happiness of a people speaking morally and religiously.' Hence 'it is very useful to consider economical questions in a purely economical point of view, in order to discover the truth respecting them merely as points of economy; although it by no means follows that what is expedient economically, is

expedient also politically, because it may well be that another end rather
than the economical may best further the attainment of the great end of
the commonwealth'.[9] So a wide gulf separated Arnold from some of the
major strands in the radicalism of his time. But if forced to choose
between conservatism and progressivism he was clear that he would
identify himself with the latter. 'No temporary evils produced by revolution shall ever make me forget the wickedness of Toryism – of that spirit
which crucified Christ Himself.'[10] Indeed, he distinguished between two
'real parties in human nature', which he labelled 'Conservatives' and
'Advancers', and he identified Christianity with the latter, 'those who
look to the future'. In a fallen world, so Arnold thought, the principle
of advancement 'must always be a true principle'.[11] And though his concept of the ethical state could have conservative implications in some
circumstances, it was in fact rooted in his progressivism. For Arnold,
whose Christianity had a distinctly Hellenized tone, the state's ethical purpose did not consist essentially in the restraint of sin. Instead, it took the
form of 'the intellectual and moral improvement of mankind, in order
to their reaching their greatest perfection, and enjoying their highest
happiness'.[12]

Maurice and Christian Socialism

F. D. Maurice (1805–72) is one of those thinkers who is difficult to place
in a synoptic study, because his influence, which was very great, was
much more extensive after his death than in his lifetime. He was an
almost exact contemporary of J. S. Mill, and at one time the two men
were close. But whereas Mill's reputation suffered in the decades after
his death, Maurice's reputation went from strength to strength. Maurice's own most systematic work belongs at the beginning of our period:
The Kingdom of Christ, which aroused little interest when first published
in 1838, and certainly much less interest than Gladstone's work on the
state and the church which appeared in the same year. Its central concern was the relationship between universal values and particular institutions, a theme at the heart of Liberal Anglican preoccupations. Its core
message was the reality of the universal church, which exists in and
through particular domestic and national institutions, so that – in
accordance with the divine constitution of man as articulated in the fact
of the incarnation – the universal was realized through the particular. 'The
Church', wrote Maurice, 'is a part, the highest part, of that spiritual constitution of which the nation and the family are lower and subordinate

parts'.[13] He was critical of universalistic secular creeds, such as Benthamism and Saint-Simonianism, for their contempt for the particular: either of these projects for constructing a universal society would, he thought, require the extinction of 'domestic feelings, associations, sympathies, all the laws by which they are upheld, all acknowledgment of relationship as a significant fact'.[14] The Benthamites, he noted, lacked any sense of nationality, and insisted on treating all *national* distinctions as mere accidents which were preferably to be discarded. Likewise they trampled over the fact that human beings live in families, that individuals are largely constituted by domestic relationships, and instead sought to found a society upon 'the hypothesis that mankind is an aggregate of individual atoms'.[15]

Maurice's understanding of the relationship between the particular societies of family and nation and the universal society of humanity was grounded (like Coleridge's) in a reading of scripture, and especially in an interpretation of the relationship between the Old Testament and the New. The old dispensation is not abrogated by the new, and hence the principles of national society articulated in God's dealings with the Jewish people were of broader significance: they provided the key to the history of all nations. 'The Father of all', he pronounced in one of his Lincoln's Inn sermons, 'does not regard special nations less, because by the birth and death of his Son, he has redeemed mankind.'[16]

What is meant by a 'nation' in this tradition of thought? The invocation of sacred history hardly implies a close affinity with modern nationalism, though it may be worth noting in this context that Seeley, who was much closer to the mainstream of nineteenth-century European nationalism, shared Coleridge's and Arnold's and Maurice's interest in the Old Testament as a source of teaching about the divine dispensation for the life of nations. Maurice wrote that the characteristics of a nation were that it had a law, a language and a government – that is, he formulated a definition which was primarily but not exclusively political.[17] But perhaps we should not dwell too much on the use of the word 'nation' here. The point of this whole discursive idiom is that it focused attention upon the significance of community in the ethical and spiritual life of man. Most nineteenth-century liberals, at least until the last decade or two of the century, were nationalists because they saw the nation as a step away from the particular and towards the universal, and not because they wished to emphasize their own nation's particularity in relation to other nations. The nation was particular in relation to other nations, but was the most general and universal of actual communities. This case was argued most vociferously by the Italian patriot Mazzini, who saw the nation as one of the key moral arenas in which we learn our duties to others. It is no surprise, therefore, to find Mazzini lionized both by mid-century Liberal Anglicans such as Jowett and by their idealist successors such as Green.

The Christian Socialists, much written about but still misunderstood, are best situated in the context of the set of Broad Church preoccupations we have described. As Christopher Harvie has observed, Christian Socialism was 'the practical embodiment of the Liberal Anglican ideal'. Maurice, their intellectual leader, was too much of an original to be easily classified, but what is not sufficiently appreciated is that the other luminaries of Christian Socialism traced their intellectual ancestry to Dr Arnold. Arnold himself was no socialist of any description, but under the impact of Chartism he was deeply moved by the 'Condition of England' question. In 1839 he wrote a series of letters to the *Hertford Reformer* calling for the formation of a non-partisan society which would set out 'to collect facts relative to the condition of the labouring classes, and to bring them to the knowledge of the public, without expressing any opinion as to the most effectual remedies for the state of things thus developed'.[18] This was an abortive project, but in a sense it was the Christian Socialist movement which realized it a decade later, though Arnold did not live to see it. Among the Christian Socialists Arnold had a powerful influence on Thomas Hughes, a pupil of his at Rugby; but also on Charles Kingsley, who resolved in 1846 to 'devote soul and body to get together an Arnoldite party of young men' whose purpose would be 'to show how all this progress of society in the present day is really of God'.[19] Likewise, J. M. Ludlow, after Maurice the most original of the Christian Socialists, found in reading Stanley's *Life of Arnold* 'a new turning point' in his intellectual development, one which launched him in the direction of Christian Socialism.

The Christian Socialist movement took shape in 1848, the year that saw ultimately abortive revolutions across continental Europe and the publication of the *Communist Manifesto*. But no-one was less revolutionary, in the political sense, than the Christian Socialists. No Christian Socialist believed in the expropriation of private property or any of the characteristic doctrines subsequently identified with European socialism. They were held together not by a political programme but by a spiritual vision: setting out from the fact of the incarnation, they saw Christ in the suffering workers of the great manufacturing towns. Thus Maurice, writing to Ludlow in the year of the European revolutions, urged 'the necessity of an English theological reformation, as the means of averting an English political revolution and of bringing what is good in foreign revolutions to know itself'.[20] At the heart of this theological reformation stood Maurice's refusal of the distinction between the sacred and the secular; and it was the force of this spiritual vision that made it difficult for the Christian Socialists to endorse a merely political programme. 'I fear all economics, politics, physics, are in danger of becoming Atheistic', explained Maurice, because all risked 'making a system which shall absolutely exclude God'. The collapse of the distinction between sacred and secular can have conservative implications; and Maurice the Christian Socialist declared in 1848 that 'property is holy, distinction of ranks is holy'.[21] Incarnationalist social criticism, seeking as it did to 'spiritualize' existing institutions and social relations, was broadly 'progressivist' in the sense that it ruled out an other-wordly attitude to social problems; but it was also establishmentarian, and thus understated the capacity of Christianity to underpin a radical criticism from without. 'A national Church must believe in the highest sense that what *is* is right', wrote Maurice in a different context.[22]

Neither Maurice nor Kingsley had much time for the 'swinish' notion of popular sovereignty, nor for the 'blasphemous' worship of public opinion. The paternalistic overtones of many of their social pronouncements leave them vulnerable to the charge, commonly levelled against them, that they were more like romantic Tories than socialists. Our ears are so attuned to the identification of Victorian Liberalism with utilitarianism that any critique of utilitarianism, unless from a radical democrat, is liable to sound like Toryism. But none of the leading Christian Socialists had any significant connection with Toryism, and this was no accident, for their Broad Churchmanship and their antipathy to doctrinally based ecclesiastical partisanship placed them much closer to the Whigs than to their opponents. The one prominent Christian Socialist to enter parliament – Thomas Hughes – sat as a Liberal. Furthermore, much as they might denounce utilitarians and Manchester radicals, Maurice and Kingsley were solidly committed to the main structure of the political economy of their day. As Kingsley wrote in 1857, political economy 'forms the subject matter of all future social science, and he who is ignorant of it builds on air'. Or in Maurice's words, when he defended his role in the co-operative movement, 'we are not setting at naught the principles of political economy, but are vindicating them from a mean and dishonourable perversion of them'.[23] As Parry and other scholars have suggested, the central features of Christian Socialism – its spiritual intensity, its educative purposes, its pursuit of the regeneration of the soul rather than the merely material reform of society – were absorbed into the mainstream of mid-Victorian Whig-Liberalism, which, in consequence, acquired a tone far removed from secular utilitarianism.[24]

Whig History and Englishness

The distinctive feature of the Arnoldian and Mauricean tradition of political thought was that it shifted attention away from narrowly political questions to the broader question of moral and spiritual reform. The nation's importance lay in its place in the moral education of man. By contrast, the distinctive characteristic of Whig history was that it placed the *constitution*, and constitutional liberty, at the centre of its account of English history and English nationhood. The development of the English nation was the principal inquiry of Victorian historians; just as, indeed, the idea of nationality and its origins was fundamental to historical inquiry throughout Europe. But what was distinctive about the Whig tradition was the articulation of nationhood in terms of constitutional liberties. 'At whatever time it originated', wrote Lord John Russell – not just a Whig historian but also, more famously, the archetypal Whig statesman – 'the early prevalence of freedom is nobly characteristic of the English nation.'[25]

Different Victorian historians constructed different narratives of the fortunes of English liberty. The Saxon scholar J. M. Kemble was convinced that the true beginnings of English national life were to be dated from the Teutonic invasions of the fifth and sixth centuries; and this notion of the Anglo-Saxon roots of English liberty was shared by many radicals – E. A. Freeman, for instance – who commonly linked it with the notion of the 'Norman yoke', the idea that the Norman Conquest had entailed the suppression of these ancient liberties. For most Whigs, by contrast, the narrative of constitutional liberty was one of progressive growth, and they were inclined to fix its birth rather later. Most homed in on the thirteenth century, and especially on Magna Carta. According to one of the most widely read popularizers of the Whig interpretation, the author of *A Text-Book of the Constitution*, E. S. Creasy, Magna Carta marked 'the commencement of our nationality'; an interesting turn of phrase, since it seems to imply not just that the distinctive quality of the English nation was its historic possession of constitutional liberty, but that, indeed, a nation cannot be a nation without some kind of common political life. Likewise Hallam and Macaulay both depicted Magna Carta as the first 'national' event. For Macaulay, King John's loss of Normandy was crucial, for it forced the Anglo-Norman nobles to identify themselves as English: 'The great grandsons of those who had fought under William and the great grandsons of those who had fought under Harold began to draw near to each other in friendship; and the first pledge of their reconciliation was the Great Charter, won by their united exertions, and framed for their common benefit.'[26] What was decisive about the thirteenth century was the appearance of the constitution in a written form, 'that constitution which has ever since, through all changes, preserved its identity; that constitution of which all the other free constitutions in the world are copies, and which, in spite of some defects, deserves to be regarded as the best under which any great society has ever yet existed during many ages'.[27] Hallam too explicitly asserted the specifically *constitutional* foundation of English character: 'the character of the bravest and most virtuous among nations has not depended on the accidents of race or climate, but has been gradually wrought by the plastic influence of civil rights, transmitted as a prescriptive inheritance through a long course of generations'.[28]

The idea of a *founding* of the English constitution and English nationality is important here: in its purest version, Whig historiography identified a point (or points) in history when English nationhood could be said to have been forged, and English liberties constituted. Their origins were not lost in the mists of time, and Whig history thus severed any connection with the ancient constitutionalists, as well as with the 'antiquarian' approach adopted by, for example, the Tory radical Toulmin Smith and the romantic liberal nationalist E. A. Freeman. The distinctive tenet of Whig history was that constitutional liberty develops and unfolds. Macaulay, after all, was a self-conscious modern Whig whose outlook was shaped by the Scottish concept of conjectural history, which he absorbed through the Edinburgh reviewers.[29] His famous third chapter, on the condition of England in 1685, emphatically underlined the extent of social, economic and moral improvement that had taken place since James II's day – 'a change to which the history of the old world furnishes no parallel' – and was thus aimed polemically at undermining the position of those who looked to the past for a golden age and a source of precedent. Likewise he did not believe that seventeenth-century England possessed an accepted 'ancient' constitution which was subverted by the Stuarts and defended by the Whigs; on the contrary, though he sometimes praised the restorative character of the Glorious Revolution, he saw its real vindication in its constitutional consequences. It inaugurated 'a new era of constitutional government' under William III, and the emergence of wholly new constitutional phenomena such as cabinet government.[30]

It is important to be clear that although many leading Whig historians were Whigs in the party sense – so that critics could accuse Macaulay of an 'air of Whig self-sufficiency' – this historiographical tradition was not narrowly partisan. Macaulay was persistently critical of the way in which both Tories and Whigs politicized history by engaging in precedent-hunting. His real thesis was that 1688 was not an exclusively Whig achievement, but that Tories and Whigs were able to act in concert to depose a tyrant. Indeed, the important thing about Whig history was that it came to constitute a sort of bipartisan orthodoxy, so that a Tory such as William Stubbs had little difficulty taking it as the framework for his historical work.

Whig history, which deployed a providential account of English history, was bound up with the notion of English exceptionalism. Her possession, by divine grace, of constitutional liberty and a continuous history marked England off from her unhappy continental rivals, subjected alternately to despotism and revolution. It was, then, a happy coincidence that two of the most famous celebrations of England's unique felicity were published in 1848, the year of European revolutions. Sir Edward Creasy's *Text Book of the Constitution* was issued sixteen times in the course of the nineteenth century. The first two volumes of Macaulay's *History of England* appeared in the same year, and immediately established the book as a bestseller. The following year saw the publication of two books articulating the conviction that English stability derived from Saxon roots: Freeman's *Thoughts on the Study of History* and Kemble's two volumes on *The Saxons in England*. Kemble – unusual among Victorian historians in having been educated at a German university – observed that, as the book was being written, 'on every side of us thrones totter, and the deep foundations of society are convulsed'. The celebration of the Jubilee of King Alfred at his birthplace, Wantage, in 1849, was effectively a celebration of the uniqueness of English liberties, and stood in contrast with the absence of any full-scale commemoration of the Battle of Hastings in 1866.

Historical knowledge was widely perceived as the basis of a distinctively political conduct. Macaulay himself was one of the most articulate Victorian commentators on the relationship between social and political change: 'The great cause of revolutions is this, that while nations move onwards, constitutions stand still.' Political action, then, was the mediator between an evolving history and inherited institutions, and revolution was the penalty for political intransigence.[31] 'It is because we had a preserving revolution in the seventeenth century', thought Macaulay, 'that we have not had a destroying revolution in the nineteenth.' It is significant that Macaulay was a great admirer of Burke, whom he considered 'the greatest man since Milton'. For Macaulay raised everyday practical experience to the status of political wisdom, and was suspicious or even contemptuous of political philosophers. He was to be reproached for this by later critics such as Morley and Leslie Stephen – both of whom, curiously enough, shared Macaulay's admiration for Burke.[32]

This Burkean account of political life was central to Whiggery. In the year of revolutions, 1848, a writer in the *Edinburgh Review* argued that stability was not the product of a 'paper constitution', but of tradition and custom; for 'that bond of custom, slight as it may seem, and absurd as it often is, is a thing omnipotent in politics'. Again: 'the law of continuity . . . and the influence of time are not accidental, but essential conditions of all political solidity'.[33] This account of the relationship between institutions and social change was to permeate mid-Victorian reformism. Two decades later it was echoed by the contributors to the Liberal *Essays on Reform*. A. O. Rutson held that 'the violent convulsion of 1789–93 was itself the result of prolonged neglect to accommodate institutions to an altered state of opinion and an altered distribution of social forces', and in the same volume James Bryce maintained: 'If there be anything which history declares to be dangerous, it is the failure to recognise a new phase of political growth.'[34] It is significant that the advanced Liberal contributors to *Essays on Reform* owed more to Whiggish historical arguments than to utilitarian deductions from the laws of human nature.

Seeley and 'National-Liberal' Historiography

The Whig version was by far the most politically potent narrative of English history for most of the Victorian period, and it yielded a politically highly usable account of English nationhood. Its political appeal, far from being confined chiefly to Whigs, in fact reached out to the radical E. A. Freeman and the Tory William Stubbs. But the Whig interpretation was visibly falling from favour by the end of our period. One of the chief agencies of the demise of Whig historiography was the work of Sir John Seeley, who used his position as Regius Professor of History at Cambridge (1869–95) to propound a new kind of national history for an imperial age. In constructing a new narrative of English history which displaced constitutionalism and liberty from their central position, Seeley set out to puncture Whig mythology. His *Expansion of England* (1883), a history of the eighteenth century which took 'the foundation of Greater Britain' as its central theme rather than the development of parliamentary government, was an enormously popular work. In the first two years after publication the book sold 80,000 copies; what is more, it was still selling well after the First World War: 11,000 copies were sold in 1919 and 3000 in 1931.[35] It did not go out of print until 1956. H. A. L. Fisher, writing shortly after Seeley's death, doubted whether 'any historical work has exercised so great an influence over the general political thinking of a nation'.[36]

Seeley was fond of presenting himself as a hard-headed political realist, dispelling the web of myth spun by lawyers, metaphysicians and moralists. He wanted to shift the focus of political science away from the metaphysical concerns of traditional political theory. 'I suggest that we should abandon for the present the enterprise of deciding what the state ought to be and to aim at, and consider by way of pure observation what it has actually been.'[37] Political science, thus conceived, would come to serve as an antidote to fanaticism, yielding 'precise and authoritative' versions of existing 'loose notions about liberty, about the province of government, about legislation and finance, about the stages of national and universal development, the relation of politics to religion'.

Rather like Bagehot, Seeley liked to present his gift as the ability to see the reality beneath the 'representation'. 'Properly speaking . . . the English parliamentary session ought not to be considered as a series of legislative debates at which the Ministers give the benefit of their official knowledge. Such a description misses the principal feature. It is a series of conferences between the executive government and the representatives of the people.' Under Seeley's assault 'the whole theory which would make Parliament the special organ of legislative power falls to the ground. For the essence of the institution appears to lie rather in some sort of negotiation or parley with the executive power'.[38] This self-conscious realism was directed in large measure against 'that Whig view of our history which has been fashionable since the time of Hallam and Macaulay', a view which exaggerated the constitutional significance of 1688 and supposed that the abeyance of royal power and the rise of the party system both dated from William III's reign.[39] Seeley thought that historians of the eighteenth century made too much of 'the mere parliamentary wrangle and the agitations about liberty, in all of which matters the eighteenth century of England was but a pale reflection of the seventeenth. They do not perceive that in that century the history of England is not in England but in America and Asia.'[40] He offered a rewriting of the English past in which the Whig emphasis on the growth of constitutional liberties was displaced by a new theme, the growth of the state, and especially the 'simple, obvious fact of the extension of the English name into the other countries of the globe, the foundation of Greater Britain'.[41] For Seeley the formative date in English history was not 1688, the year of the Glorious Revolution, but 1588, the year of the defeat of the Armada.

Seeley was, however, no mere propagandist for imperial power politics. He did not wish to strip politics of its ethical content. On the contrary – and this is why he is doubly relevant for our story – he was a Broad Churchman whose rehabilitation of the state drew less on Bismarck than on Thomas Arnold. He first achieved celebrity as the author of one of the most famous religious books of the century, *Ecce Homo*, the best-known of the numerous Victorian lives of Jesus. Published anonymously, the book was received in horror by the evangelicals among whom Seeley had been raised; but it was also greatly admired by many churchmen, especially by exponents of the 'social gospel'. It was praised, for instance, by the High Churchman Charles Gore and the theological modernist Hastings Rashdall.

In an important lecture on 'The Church as a teacher of morality', Seeley insisted that 'morals cannot be severed from politics any more than the individual can be isolated from society', and he always viewed the nation-state as an ethical force rather than as a power standing above morality. The nation was a sphere in which the individual was lifted out of and above mere parochial and tribal loyalties towards something higher. And though Seeley's religious faith seems not to have long survived the controversies aroused by this work, his moral concerns – now channelled through the largely secular Ethical Society movement – continued to underpin his work. He was unusually explicit about the moral and political purposes he attributed to history. Moral virtue, he urged, should be inculcated by the study of national history and the commemoration of the deeds of our great ancestors: 'we should form, as it were, a national calendar, consecrate our ancestors – keep their images near to us'.[42] Seeley was the most vocal British advocate of history as civic religion, of the kind that underpinned the ideological project of French republicans in the 1880s.

Seeley's Liberal Anglican background and continuing concern with the ethical basis of politics shaped the way in which he defined the central problem of political science and history, which he took to be the problem of *identity*: the 'fundamental fact ... that men should conceive themselves as belonging, and belonging in such an intimate and momentous union, to a corporation which is not simply the family'. The influence of Thomas Arnold and Maurice could be traced in his repudiation of the attempts of political economists and utilitarians to produce an account of social cohesion and political obligation based on interest. 'The English state', he thought, 'may be held together in some degree by a common interest, still it is not a mere company composed of voluntary shareholders, but a union which has its root in the family, and which has grown, and not merely been arranged, to be what it is.'[43]

This underlying concern with identity as the foundation of political and social cohesion shaped the way in which Seeley thought about 'Greater Britain', especially in his greatest historical work *The Expansion of England*. He drew a sharp distinction between the Indian empire on the one hand and the colonial empire (meaning the white Dominions) on the other. The distinctive characteristic of the former was that its population was 'of alien race and religion', and bound to England only by conquest. The latter, by contrast, could form a true political community with England, for their populations 'are of our own blood, and are therefore united with us by the strongest tie'. While he was sceptical, therefore, of the value of the possession of India, which 'vastly increases our dangers and responsibilities', he took a very different view of the colonial empire. There were, he thought, three bonds which held states together: community of race, community of religion, and community of interest. 'By the first two our colonies are evidently bound to us, and this fact by itself makes the connection strong. It will grow indissolubly firm if we come to recognise also that interest bids us to maintain the connection, and this conviction seems to gain ground. When we inquire then into the Greater Britain of the future we ought to think much more of our Colonial than of our Indian Empire.'[44] It was this recognition of the importance of interest as a political bond that provided the inspiration for the 'constructive imperialists' who, after Seeley's death, gave intellectual ballast to Joseph Chamberlain's tariff reform campaign.[45]

In Seeley we can trace the redefinition of national identity in the context of Britain's changing place in the world. Imperial and geopolitical problems of various kinds impinged increasingly on political thought in the Victorian period, within a number of different intellectual traditions. India was central to the concerns of the two Mills, both of whom served for many years as officials of the East India Company, and of their antagonist Macaulay, who presided over the drafting of a criminal law code for the sub-continent. Later, the distinctive problems of governing India influenced the very different styles of thought of the neo-Hobbesian utilitarian Sir James Fitzjames Stephen and the evolutionary historicist Sir Henry Maine. Much the same could be said of Ireland. Dicey's emphasis on parliamentary sovereignty as the cornerstone of the constitution was deployed polemically as a weapon in the struggle against Home Rule, for the implicit adoption of a federal model of empire would unleash inexorable pressure for a written constitution which would limit the supremacy of parliament. From a very different point of view, the challenge posed to classical economics by the historical school owed a great deal to the clash between the abstract model of economic man and the reality of agrarian custom in Ireland. Significantly, two of the pioneers of the historical school of economics were the Irishmen T. E. Cliffe Leslie and J. K Ingram: the former was a pupil of Maine and was greatly influenced by his mentor's study of *Village Communities* (1871). This whole subject would merit closer historical investigation.

Religion and Identity

So far I have argued that the Broad Church or Liberal Anglican tradition was fertile soil for Victorian reflection about nationality; and that in this whole discourse there was an intimate relationship between nationality and religion. Gladstone, though he was always an Anglican and became a Liberal, was no Liberal Anglican: to him dogma was always of the essence of religion, and he detested any suggestion of the supremacy of the civil power in church matters. But he stood at the centre of Victorian discussions of the relationship between nationality and religion, and he articulated an original and (in its way) compelling position on the issues that concerned Coleridge and Maurice, Arnold and Newman.

What made Gladstone a High Churchman, in defiance of his evangelical upbringing, was his growing emphasis in the 1830s on the corporate nature of the church, his disenchantment with the individualism of the evangelical tradition in which he was brought up – in a word, his grow-ing sense of *catholicity*. This sense, first aroused by his visit to Rome in 1832, was articulated in his first book *The State in its Relations with the Church* (1838), in which his purpose was to expound and defend the political theory of ecclesiastical establishment in its full integrity, and to relate it to an important theory of the relationship between religion and nationality. The nation-state was, for Gladstone, a moral organism; but a spiritual element – religious belief – was a defining feature of a nation, and national life was 'curtailed in its moral fulness' insofar as it lacked 'the clear and intelligible profession of unity in faith and in commu-nion'.[46] The national church constituted, so to speak, the conscience of the nation-state; indeed, in open rebellion against the evangelicalism of his upbringing, Gladstone at this stage went so far as to deny that con-science could be individual at all. The 'master idea' of the book – as Glad-stone summarized it thirty years later, was 'that the State as it then stood was capable in this age, as it had been in ages long gone by, of assuming beneficially a responsibility for the inculcation of a particular religion'.[47]

The book was savaged by Macaulay in a review which, conceding that Gladstone had propounded 'an original theory on a great problem in politics', maintained that its doctrines were 'in the highest degree perni-cious', and that if implemented they 'would inevitably produce the dis-solution of society'.[48] For the state to take it upon itself to propagate religious truth would alienate nonconformists and limit the supply of able men for the service of the state, and thus hamper its capacity to fulfil its primary objects as a civil association, the maintenance of civil peace and public order.[49]

But it was not Macaulay's critique that dislodged Gladstone from his theoretical position, for Gladstone felt he had satisfactorily answered that critique in amendments to later editions; rather, it was the exigen-cies of political reality which he experienced as a minister in Peel's second government. His famous, and to many contemporaries baffling, resignation from the cabinet over the Maynooth grant – the renewal of the state grant to a Roman Catholic educational institution in Ireland – had the purpose of giving him the moral freedom to rethink his position on a proposal manifestly at odds with his published views, but which he now considered politically compelling.

It would be a mistake, however, to suppose that Gladstone ever fully recanted his early views. Even as he moved towards an enthusiastic championing of the idea of religious liberty, he never regretted publish-ing his book of 1838. For at its heart stood a conviction – integral to his churchmanship – which he never abandoned: his lively sense of the catholicity of the church, and his 'high' doctrine of the place of the church in the economy of salvation. He defended the book in retrospect on the ground of the contribution it had made to the retreat of those views (dominant in the eighteenth century) which considered the church a mere instrument of state policy. His book was, he recalled at the end of his life, 'the first manifestation from a political quarter of what was eventually to be a revolution in political opinion. It was anti-Erastian from beginning to end.'[50]

In the decade or so after Maynooth, a series of issues – university reform, for instance, and the admission of dissenters to parliament – persuaded Gladstone that the integrally Anglican establishment could no longer be maintained. As he reached this judgement, he came to the view that the maintenance of the pretence that the state had a role in the promotion of religion would lead relentlessly to the encroachment on the corporate integrity of the church. Since he loathed Erastianism and looked with dismay upon Whiggish attempts to preserve the Anglican character of the state by diluting the content of Anglican doctrine, the conclusion was clear: disestablishment was the only way, in the long run, of preserving the freedom and integrity of the church.

Gladstone nevertheless had much in common with the Liberal Anglican tradition; notably his concept of religious nationality which approximated at times to that of Coleridge and Arnold. He read Coleridge's *Constitution of Church and State* in 1837 – seven years after its first publication – and noted it carefully. Conversely, in his inaugural lecture Dr Arnold saw the author of *The State in its Relations with the Church* as a sort of ally. In the 1830s Gladstone had come to believe, first, that there is what he called 'a real and not merely suppositious personality of nations, which entails likewise its own religious responsibilities'; and secondly that the Church of England represented (in England, Wales, Ireland and the colonies, though not in Scotland) the 'religious responsibility' of the state – the responsibility of determining what the disposition of a good citizen should be.[51]

But the fundamental question is how far this notion of religious nationality survived the crisis of the 1840s – the crisis of the Church, with the secession of Newman, and the crisis of the state, with the Maynooth grant. In the immediate aftermath of the crisis Gladstone exaggerated the extent to which moralized politics were now impossible. He told Newman in 1845 that 'the State cannot be said now to have a conscience ... inasmuch as I think it acts ... as no conscience – that is, no personal conscience (which is the only real form of one) – can endure'. But he stayed in politics, as he explained to Stanley, because 'the lower ends of a State ought to be fulfilled even when the higher ones should have become impractical'. Or, as he told Manning, he was now engaged in a 'process of lowering the religious tone of the State, letting it down, demoralizing it – i.e., stripping it of its ethical character, and assisting its transition into one which is mechanical'.

But this talk about stripping the state of its ethical character may have been a short-term reaction to a crisis in his political thinking. In many ways Gladstone retained a thoroughly organic conception of the state, and retained a belief in the vital contribution of religion to national identity. Colin Matthew has argued that Gladstone came to see free trade as 'the class-integrating factor in the organic state' – a substitute for his system of Church and State – and that he came to invest free trade with the moral role in the nation's ethical progress which he had earlier attributed to the established church.[52] In the *apologia* he wrote in 1868, he referred to the emancipation of trade and industry as 'the accomplishment of another great and blessed work of public justice'.[53]

For all his oecumenism, Gladstone never lost his great admiration for the Reformation, and especially for the assertion of English nationality entailed in the Henrician Reformation. He saw the Church of England as the embodiment of (universal) religion for the English nation. 'The nationality of religion is conducive to the realisation of this intended universality, and, consequently, the renunciation of the first [national religion] is unfavourable to the attainment of the second [universality].' In *The State in its Relations with the Church* he held that the establishment was justified on the ground that it helped attract to religion the power of nationality, and thus strengthened religion. Though he abandoned his belief in establishment, he held to an underlying belief in religious nationality. As he wrote in 1875:

> Attached to my own religious communion, the Church of my birth and my country, I have never loved it with a merely sectional or insular attachment, but have thankfully regarded it as that portion of the great redeemed Christian family in which my lot had been cast – not by, but for me.[54]

A positive relationship between liberty and nationality was taken for granted by most Victorian liberals, and was argued most explicity by J. S. Mill in Chapter 16 of his *Considerations on Representative Government*

(1861). Mill recognized that one of the defects of Benthamism was its inability to offer a credible account of the conditions for political stability, and in this work he sought to make good this fault. 'Free institutions', he argued, 'are next to impossible in a country made up of different nationalities', because a multinational state can hardly possess the sort of united public opinion that is the necessary complement of liberal government.[55] This was not an implausible position, and it was broadly in tune with the beliefs of most liberals in nineteenth-century Europe, at least before nationalism took a rightward turn towards the end of the century. But it did receive one influential rebuttal, from the historian Lord Acton. Acton was the most prominent Catholic intellectual and publicist in Victorian England; he was also a liberal, and a man of wide European culture; and these three perspectives informed the account of nationality he gave in a well-known article of 1862.

The central theme in Acton's political thought was the threat posed to freedom by the concentration of power within the state. Just as he saw religious pluralism as an important protection for liberty, so he maintained that 'the coexistence of several nations under the same state is a test, as well as the best security, of its freedom'.[56] He also thought multinationalism a soure of progress, for he shared the view of many nineteenth-century liberals – Guizot, Mill, Bagehot – that diversity was the best guarantee of innovation and vitality, whereas homogeneity tended to produce stagnation. 'It is in the cauldron of the state that the fusion takes place by which the vigour, the knowledge, and the capacity of one portion of mankind may be communicated to another. Where political and national boundaries coincide, society ceases to advance, and nations relapse into a condition corresponding to that of men who renounce intercourse with their fellow-men.'[57]

Culture and Democracy: Matthew Arnold versus Bagehot

Though the Victorians rarely used the noun 'intellectual' in its modern sense, the intellectuals of the high Victorian age were increasingly conscious of their standing as intellectuals, and one of their central concerns was with the social role of intellectuals – or, put in other terms, with the problem of cultural authority in a democratic age, with the relationship between 'brains' and 'numbers'. What was the relationship between two of the most salient features of the age: intellectual progress on the one hand, and the growth of democracy on the other? The problem of 'democracy' was understood in terms of culture as well as in terms of political institutions. The greater self-consciousness and cohesion of the intelligentsia of the time was reflected in groups such as the Metaphysical Society, which included in its membership the cream of the intellectual life of the age. It was deeply involved in reflection upon these problems.

Matthew Arnold was the Victorian thinker most closely identified with the discussion of this problem. Like Mill, he sought to present himself as an outsider, berating the complacent insularity of his fellow-countrymen and invoking the authority of continental (especially French) thought and practice; and he was unusual in his explicit invocation of the role of the state. But it is important to see that Arnold was contributing to a debate which was central to the concerns of contemporary intellectuals, especially in the era of the 1867 Reform Act, which was widely perceived as instituting a democratic political system. He was not unusual but in a sense quite typical in coupling the problem of democracy with the problem of cultural authority. Furthermore, Arnold is not out of place in a study of Victorian *political* thought. It is true, of course, that he is much better known to students of English literature than to political theorists, and that his political thought was neither strikingly original nor (given his aversion to conflict) particularly persuasive; but it was intimately connected with his cultural theory. His most famous work, *Culture and Anarchy*, was subtitled 'an essay in political and social criticism'; and that fact itself suggests how artificial it would be to fence off Arnold's standing as a critic from his position as a political thinker. He was engaged with politics *because* he was a critic. This is a point he made explicit in his lecture on 'Numbers, or the majority and the remnant', delivered in 1883. There he noted that matters such as culture and morality do not normally come to mind in discussions of politics. 'But the philosophers and prophets maintain that these matters, and not those of which the heads of politicians are full, do really govern politics and save or destroy states. They save or destroy them by a salient inexorable fatality; while the politicians are making believe, plausibly and noisily, with their American institutions, British Constitution, and civilising mission of France.'[58]

Arnold is often, and with good reason, held to have developed a critique of the values of the provincial middle classes who formed the backbone of Victorian Liberalism; and it is no accident that *Culture and Anarchy* begins with a quotation from 'that fine speaker and famous Liberal', John Bright, which disparages preachers of culture. But the concern with cultural authority was by no means primarily a conservative preoccupation. Like his father, Arnold always defined himself as a liberal, though with qualifications: 'a Liberal tempered by experience, reflection, and renouncement'. And the critique he developed was a *liberal* critique of Victorian liberalism. It mobilized a central notion in Victorian liberal thought, namely the primacy of the national as opposed to the merely sectional, and turned it against what he saw as the excesses of provincial nonconformity. He contested (but also exaggerated) the predominantly negative view of the state which was typical of a certain kind of Victorian liberal, and instead of deprecating state action as such, he sought to elevate the state so that it might come to represent 'our best self'. He clearly identified with the cause of liberal reform, which, to the Victorians, meant the reordering of important social institutions (schools or universities, cathedral chapters or municipal corporations) to make them serve truly 'national' purposes.

Arnold's cultural critique of the values of the provincial middle class was bound up with a critique of democracy. He identified democracy with the primacy of the 'lower self', of unstable, unpredictable, animal instincts; and for Arnold, a quintessential hellenist, the unstable and changing was bad and the static and harmonious was good. Accepting Tocqueville's sociological thesis that society was moving inexorably towards democracy and equality,[59] Arnold maintained that, precisely because it was inevitable, democracy would have to be tempered by the entrenchment of culture: 'We must insist on the urgent necessity, in the reign of democratic ideas, of maintaining or of building up the culture of the spirit as a counter-weight to the brutality and violence which is their natural bent.'[60]

In the mid-Victorian period a good number of intellectuals were facing up to the need to shore up cultural authority in response to the advent of democracy. One response was the campaign for the 'endowment of research', which attracted high-powered support from such notable luminaries in the Victorian intellectual galaxy as Pattison, Seeley and Sidgwick. In an age of intellectual ferment, the process of independent and active inquiry – of 'research' – needed to be given some sort of authoritative standing by being defined as the central function of the university. Intellectual and cultural authority could no longer take the form of a simple defence of a patrimony, but must entail the active extension and enlargement and indeed questioning of that patrimony. In a sense Arnold's endorsement of the cultural role of academies, for which his model was the Académie Française, was a simple variant of the case for the endowment of research in universities. In a famous essay published in 1864, Arnold traced the superiority of French prose style to the existence of 'a recognised authority, imposing on us a high standard in matters of intellect and taste'. The French Academy acted as 'a sort of centre and rallying-point' for educated opinion; and, furthermore, as 'a sovereign organ of the highest literary opinion, a recognised authority in matters of intellectual tone and taste'.[61]

It goes without saying that the search for a source of cultural authority capable of acting as a counterweight to the advance of democracy was not universally accepted. It was associated with those who, like Arnold, saw the spectre of anarchy behind the growth of democratic politics, and who thought that the restlessness of the age was an aberrant phenomenon. Yet Arnold's mentor, Tocqueville – the single most important authority in Victorian debates about democracy – could be invoked to support a very different interpretation: the chief threat posed by democracy was not that of social disintegration but that of stagnation; and from that point of view the Arnoldian quest for cultural authority might exacerbate the problem rather than alleviating it. This was the position adopted by J. S. Mill, who declined to associate himself with the campaign for the endowment of research, maintaining instead that 'experience shows that Academies whether of literature or science generally prefer inoffensive mediocrities to men of original genius'.[62] Perhaps the foremost exponent of this outlook, however, was Walter Bagehot, who like Mill was quite clearly influenced by Tocqueville. Bagehot is one of the best known of Victorian political writers, but would not normally be read alongside Matthew Arnold, and this juxtaposition therefore needs some elaboration.

Bagehot is chiefly read nowadays for *The English Constitution*, which in spite of much criticism still commands the status of a classic. There Bagehot set out to puncture what he took to be the reigning myths about the way in which Britain was governed, and principally the 'literary theory' of the consitution, with its twin obsolete doctrines, the theory of mixed government and the theory of the separation of powers. Instead, Bagehot maintained that the essential principle of the English constitution was the *fusion* of legislative and executive powers in the hands of the cabinet, itself a committee of the House of Commons. The House of Commons was thus not simply a legislative body, but a *ruling* body: indeed, it was because it effectively decided who was to govern that its deliberations were of such interest and importance. Cabinet government was the 'efficient secret' of the constitution, and Bagehot drew his famous distinction between the 'dignified' and the 'efficient' parts of the constitution; the former (notably the monarchy) being important sources of legitimacy even though they were not working institutions.

The English Constitution has had the misfortune to be left to constitutionalists rather than being read alongside Bagehot's other (voluminous) writings. His most intellectually ambitious work, *Physics and Politics*, was a major contribution to mid-Victorian social theory, not least because it was one of the earliest attempts to work out the implications of Darwinism for social thought. Here Bagehot engaged with both Matthew and Thomas Arnold as two of his leading antagonists. The book also had an important place, now quite forgotten, in the wider European intellectual world, since it was translated into seven languages and had an unmistakable though unacknowledged influence on French social thinkers such as Gabriel Tarde and Gustave Le Bon. Bagehot was dismissive of the Arnoldian quest for entrenched intellectual authority, just as he was dismissive of the Comtean concept of the 'spiritual power'. Positivists and Arnoldians alike set out to impose the kind of centralized discipline which, useful in the early stages of civilization, thereafter risked stifling the potential for progress. Arnold, he warned, 'wants to put a yoke upon us – and, worse than a political yoke, an academic yoke, a yoke upon our minds and our styles'. The institution of academies, on the French model, as centres of cultural authority, would tend to stultify intellectual and literary growth, for 'the academies are asylums of the ideas and the tastes of the last age'.[63] Bagehot's priority was the same as that of Sir Henry Maine in *Ancient Law*: to explain why European nations alone had displayed the progressive genius that allowed them to free themselves from the 'cake of custom'. Echoing Darwin's concept of random mutations, he identified variation and diversity as the seeds of progress, and concluded that Arnold's high concept of culture was antagonistic to diversity and hence to progress. Bagehot was himself no democrat; but he was right to see Arnold as an enemy of his point of view, for Arnold's whole cast of mind was shot through with a nostalgia for a static, harmonious world, and in Arnold's critique of democracy, it has been well said, can be found a sort of agoraphobia induced by the historical relativism of the time.[64]

Bagehot's cast of thought, by contrast, was dynamic. His critique of the Arnoldian understanding of cultural authority rested upon a repudiation of the static view of the foundations of communal cohesion. In *Physics and Politics* he made a fundamental distinction between the factors that made for cohesion – or 'nation-making' – and those that facilitated progress. The error of the Arnoldians lay in their failure to realize that factors such as common religious beliefs, which were important in the first process, could stifle the second, which relied upon 'discussion', rather than authority.[65]

'Government by discussion' was a central theme in Bagehot's political writings. In *Physics and Politics* he identified 'discussion' as the defining quality of modernity and the condition of progress, for 'a government by discussion, if it can be borne, at once breaks down the yoke of fixed custom'.[66] But it was also the characteristic quality of parliamentary government, as he identified it. 'A Parliamentary Government', he wrote, 'is essentially a Government by discussion; by constant speaking and writing a public opinion is formed which decides on all action and all policy.'[67] This was not true of either consultative or presidential government. The antithesis between cabinet or parliamentary government on the one hand and presidential government on the other was a rhetorically and substantively powerful component of his argument in *The English Constitution*. There he identified 'critical opposition' as a decisive quality of cabinet government, in which the legislative assembly became 'the great engine of popular instruction and political controversy'. Hence his dictum that 'Cabinet government educates the nation; the presidential does not educate it, and may corrupt it.'[68] The exclusion of the minister from the legislature in a presidential system removed much of the incentive for men of ability to seek a legislative mandate, and so brought about 'the degradation of public life'.[69] In other words, it was the fact that the House of Commons was a ruling as well as a legislative body that made it such a powerful instrument for the political education of the nation.

Bagehot has been variously claimed as a conservative and as a Whig. In fact both interpretations depend heavily on the incontestably Burkean strand running through his thought. But this is not enough to place Bagehot politically, for Burke was the universal hero of the Victorian political mind, cherished by Whigs, conservatives and modern-minded liberals alike. Many of his Victorian admirers belonged squarely in the non-Whig strands of the liberal tradition: this was true of Leslie Stephen and John Morley, but above all of Gladstone, who first read and absorbed Burke when at Oxford and was still reading him daily in the midst of political crisis in 1885, when he opined that Burke's work was 'sometimes almost divine', and 'what a magazine of wisdom on Ireland and America'.[70]

What Victorians absorbed above all from Burke's teaching was a sense of the dynamic tension between inherited institutions and social change.

The former were to be cherished, were not to be allowed to ossify in such a way as to become unresponsive to legitimate demands for change; for otherwise revolution would result. Burke's 'great step in political philosophy' was, in Bagehot's words, that he 'first taught the world at large . . . that politics are made of time and place – that institutions are shifting things, to be tried by and adjusted to the shifting conditions of a mutable world – that, in fact, politics are but a piece of business – to be determined in every case by the exact exigencies of that case; in plain English – by sense and circumstances'.[71]

The problems of cultural authority and the Burkean inheritance were both intimately bound up with a problem which, though of central and abiding concern to the Victorian political mind, has yet to benefit from extended treatment by historians of ideas. This is the relation between law and opinion. This problem was to structure Dicey's famous lectures on Victorian public policy (1905); and Dicey's book, with its pivotal dichotomy of individualism and collectivism, was itself to shape subsequent interpretations of Victorian political thought.

The problem of the relations between law and policy on the one hand, and public opinion on the other, was of crucial importance to the liberal mind. Keith Baker has observed that the term 'opinion publique' emerged in late eighteenth-century France as a 'central rhetorical figure in a new kind of politics'. It constituted a 'new source of authority'.[72] But if the concept emerged first in France, it was in Britain that the practice of the new politics flourished, as in the years following the peace of 1815 middle-class values became so widespread that they could no longer be ignored by government and legislature. A landmark was a book published by W. A. Mackinnon, *On the Rise, Progress, and Present State of Public Opinion* (1828). Mackinnon defined public opinion as 'that sentiment on any given subject which is entertained by the best informed, most intelligent, and most moral persons in the community' and 'gradually adopted by nearly all persons of any education or proper feeling'. Its growth depended upon 'information, proper religious feeling, facility of communication and capital'. As Parry has shown, the term 'liberal' was brought into common currency by politicians such as Canning in the same decade, to denote 'mild' and flexible policies to avert the advent of 'a great struggle between property and population'.[73] A liberal was one who did not believe that the authority of government could hold out against the settled convictions of public opinion, but who maintained that political leadership was about negotiating the interaction between them.

The belief that the dialectic of authority and opinion structured modern politics was to become something of a settled conviction of Victorian liberals as they came to see growth and change as normal features of modern political life. Bagehot saw this more clearly than most. He argued that liberalism – with which he identified – consisted in a quest for equilibrium between the 'predominance of the politically intelligent' and the 'gradual training of the politically unintelligent'.[74] Elsewhere he was more explicit about the liberal's assumption of the continuing evolution of the political order: he defined liberalism as 'the faith in the possibility, nay the duty, of constant political expansion – of drawing a larger and larger portion of the population into the circle of political duties which connect them with the government, give them a control over it, and interest them in what it does'.[75]

It was appropriate, then, that the pre-eminent Liberal leader of the Victorian age should have formulated a distinctive and characteristically subtle treatment of the relationship between political leadership and public opinion. Gladstone's *Chapter of Autobiography* was written in 1868 in defence of his decision to back the disestablishment of the Irish church in apparent defiance of his previous writings. The problem of consistency on the part of statesmen had changed in character in the nineteenth century, Gladstone argued, because of the mobility of public opinion – 'the movement of the public mind', he considered, had been 'of a nature entirely transcending former experience'; and because that movement had been 'more promptly and more effectively represented, than at any earlier period, in the action of the Government and the Legislature'.[76]

The relationship between the statesman and public opinion must be complex and dialectical, to Gladstone's mind. The statesman must 'take account of the facts in which he is to work'; he should certainly strive 'to elevate the standard of opinion and action around him', but should not seek to build a utopia. His business was 'to conduct the affairs of a living and working community of men, who have self-government recognised as in the last resort the moving spring of their political life, and of the institutions which are its outward vesture'. He saw he was living in an age marked by a new kind of politics, characterized by 'the gradual transfer of political power from groups and limited classes to the community, and the constant seething of the public mind, in fermentation upon a vast mass of moral and social, as well as merely political, interests'.[77]

The significance of Maynooth, coming on top of the repeal of the Tests Act and Catholic Emancipation, was that 'the state has ceased to stand in a relation of authority towards the people, but has become an organ of the popular will'. In such a situation, where 'the community itself is split and severed into opinions and communions', it was pointless to strive to prop up the establishment. What was crucial to Gladstone, writing in 1868, was that in spite of the relaxation of the 'dogmatic allegiance of the State to religion', the state's 'consciousness of moral duty' had been 'notably quickened and enhanced'.[78]

The dialectic of legislation and opinion ran through Bagehot's works too, though he preferred to speak of 'the accordance in opinion between Parliament and the nation'. This was, as Gertrude Himmelfarb has noted, one manifestation of a motif which ran through Bagehot's writings: the double nature of man.[79] In his writings on parliamentary reform in the 1850s and 1860s he showed no sympathy for the view that parliament should provide an exact reflection of the composition or opinion of the nation. He was, however, anxious that parliament should not be at odds with the dynamics of national life. The counties, he argued, enjoyed excessive representation vis-à-vis the boroughs: not in the sense that the county population per member was smaller than that of the boroughs (it was not), but because the borough electorate was growing more rapidly, and 'in the long run, public opinion will be much more influenced by the growing portion of the country than by the stationary'.[80]

The role of the political leader, then, was to steer a judicious course between following the lead of public opinion, and seeking to shape that opinion:

A real statesman at the present day must endeavour to enlarge the influence of the growing parts of the nation, as compared with the stationary; to augment the influence of the capitalist classes, but to withstand the pernicious theories which some of them for the moment advocate; to organise an expression for the desires of the lower orders, but to withstand even the commencement of a democratic revolution.[81]

For Bagehot this tension between statesman and populace, between political wisdom and the commonplaces of public opinion, was a potentially fruitful and dynamic tension, which had the power to generate progress. This was J. S. Mill's position too. Mill initially followed Coleridge and the Saint-Simonians in valuing the 'general power of knowledge and cultivated intelligence' as a source of intellectual authority necessary for the preservation of social order. But he later came to conceive of the role of intellectuals like himself in rather different terms: they were to provide 'a great social support for opinions and sentiments different from those of the mass'. In an increasingly democratic age they could help maintain the 'perpetual antagonism which has kept the human mind alive'.

The tension between leadership and public opinion was also a central theme in a work which was roughly contemporaneous with *Culture and Anarchy* and *Physics and Politics*: namely *Order and Progress* (1875), by the leading English positivist, Frederic Harrison. The three works belong together in the sense that, as Harrison's biographer has remarked, 'all sought to find a centre of authority in social thought'.[82] Harrison's book was more directly concerned with political institutions than were the other two; but like both Bagehot and Arnold he was persuaded that political theory raised questions that went much deeper than mere institutional questions. Indeed, he argued that the power of suffrage reform to effect change had been greatly exaggerated both by its supporters and by its enemies. On the one hand, Harrison was a reformer, and in a thinly veiled attack on Arnold he repudiated 'that political quietism which seems to be the note of sundry minor Prophets of Culture'. On the other hand he firmly sided with the party of authority against what he labelled the party of anarchy.[83]

The main theme of *Order and Progress* was the need to reconcile opposing principles: not just the two positivist catchwords cited in the title, but also, more immediately, the 'principle of authority' and the 'principle of opinion'. Harrison located the crisis of the age in the tension between the idea that government belongs exclusively to special capacity and the idea that government must emanate from the collective will of the nation.[84] He recognized the growing ascendancy of public opinion as one of the salient developments of the age; but he also identified it, if unchecked, as an anarchical development. For the reconciliation of these two principles he looked to the capable statesman, such as Abraham Lincoln, who could on the one hand act as the organ of public opinion, and on the other hand lead and mould that opinion.[85] Harrison saw this as the central problem of modern politics.

> The modern statesman [he wrote] has to be for ever modifying public opinion, and to be for ever modified by it. He must strain every nerve to carry the right measure to completion, short of the point where it meets with fixed and invincible opposition. He must never force, and never be forced. He must create the opinion on which alone he rests for strength – create it by honestly forcing the conviction that he is

right, not by manipulating electoral strings. The body on which he works is as changeful as the sea; yet it has currents as irresistible as the tide. But he is as little to be carried hither and thither by the breath of every wind as he is to brace himself to beat back the set of the tide.[86]

Assumptions about the progressiveness of man and society structured debates about parliamentary reform in the era of the second and third Reform Acts of 1867 and 1884. Whereas reform in 1832 had commonly been defended as a once-and-for-all change which would avert the need for further extensions of the suffrage, the assumption that underlay the debates of the 1860s was that the political system was almost by definition in a state of permanent flux. Most liberal intellectuals, such as the contributors to *Essays on Reform* (1867), welcomed the broadening of the political nation, not just because they believed that urban workers had demonstrated their political maturity, but also because they held that the question of reform had to be considered dynamically. Since man's higher qualities are developed by being used, the best way to ensure the civic education of the working class was to give them the vote.[87]

This is not to say that the prospect of democracy was welcomed. One of the factors that precipitated the flight of intellectuals from liberalism towards conservatism around the 1880s was a sense that progress, which was necessarily precarious, flourished best in conditions of equilibrium and diversity in which no one class was dominant. The advent of 'democracy' – widely assumed to have arrived by 1884 – was expected to produce the kind of social homogeneity that would stifle progress. This argument was central to Robert Lowe's case against the extension of the franchise in 1867. Lowe maintained that the strength of the British constitution lay in its complexity, but that the advent of something like householder suffrage in the boroughs would upset the delicate 'balance of classes' that was the best guarantee of the progressiveness of the political system. Unlike the contributors to *Essays on Reform*, he was oblivious to arguments based on the supposedly educative consequences of political participation: for Lowe, the issue had to turn on the impact of different franchises on the practice of parliamentary government. The 1867 Act would lead to the 'swamping' of other classes by the urban working class. This point of view was shared by political writers of the calibre of Sir Henry Maine and A. V. Dicey, Henry Sidgwick and Sir James Fitzjames Stephen: men who thought themselves faithful adherents of a classical liberal orthodoxy which was in danger of being trampled under foot by the onward march of democracy.

3

THE DISCOVERY OF SOCIETY: EVOLUTION, ETHICS AND THE STATE

Historians have often suggested that the foundations of social and political thought were transformed in the late Victorian period by the growing ascendancy of the natural sciences in the aftermath of the 'Darwinian revolution'. This revolution is said to have made static conceptions of human nature and society untenable, and under its impact contractual gave way to organic accounts of the state. Organicism in its turn is said to have provided the ideological foundation for the rise of the collectivist state under the influence of New Liberals, Fabians and others. In this chapter I want to sound a sceptical note. Of course it is unquestionable that the language of politics in the late-Victorian and Edwardian periods was saturated with evolutionary and organic metaphors. But these metaphors sprang from a variety of sources, of which the biological sciences were just one, and they could as easily underpin individualist as collectivist approaches to public policy. The social and political thought of the period was characterized not by the hegemony of the natural sciences, but by the dialectical interaction of scientific and ethical impulses. 'Science' and 'ethics' stood in a relationship of dynamic tension, as Beatrice Webb observed in her survey of the period of her intellectual formation. She identified two key tenets which were held in harness. The first was belief in scientific method, or 'that intellectual synthesis of observation and experiment, hypothesis and verification, by means of which alone all mundane problems were to be solved'. But the scientific method was not self-sufficient, because it 'did not yield the purpose of life'. It therefore had to be twinned with the second tenet, which she defined as 'the consciousness of a new motive; the transference of the emotion of self-sacrificing service from God to man'; in short, an ethical impulse to the service of humanity.[1] It was the interaction of the scientific ascendancy and the obsessive preoccupation with ethics that gave this period its distinctive intellectual atmosphere.

The first point to make about the relationship between natural science and social theory is that the influence was by no means exclusively in one direction. In particular it is difficult to pin down a Darwinian revolution in social theory following hard on the heels of a Darwinian revolution in the biological sciences. It is well known, for instance, that Darwin's reading of political economy, and especially the works of Malthus, suggested to him the mechanism by which evolution of species occurred, namely natural selection in the context of a struggle for existence. This was a case of intellectual transfer from the social to the natural sciences. Neither was hegemonic; rather, they shared a 'common context'.[2]

Furthermore, 'Darwinism' was rarely transferred *en bloc* from the biological sciences to social and political theory, even by self-proclaimed Darwinians such as Herbert Spencer. Victorian social thinkers in fact found Darwin's understanding of the mechanism of evolution far less fruitful, when applied to the study of society, than the Lamarckian concept of the heritability of acquired characteristics, which having been acquired by one generation subsequently entered the genetic make-up of the species. This was chiefly because the Lamarckian account buttressed some of the most cherished moral assumptions of the period, especially those concerning the profound ethical signficance of habit for the progress or degeneration of character. So an account of the relationship between natural science and social and political thought should attend not only to the 'authority' of natural scientists, but also, and more importantly, to the political uses of concepts and metaphors drawn from the sciences. After all, the 'influence' of natural science on social and political thought really consisted of some rather promiscuous borrowing of concepts, and the important question for historians to ask is why political thinkers found certain scientific concepts helpful while preferring to ignore others. The inherent authority of the sciences plainly does not provide the answer.

Organicism, Social Evolution and the State

Since Newton's time, political thinkers had liked to analyse the state as a mechanism. This approach focused attention on the origins of the state, and gave credibility to contractarian accounts of those origins. In the nineteenth century, as the biological sciences came to the fore as the field in which the most innovative scientific work was being done, the organic analogy acquired popularity. 'In the present age the most conspicuously advancing science is biology', wrote the New Liberal philosopher D. G. Ritchie; 'and the categories of organism and evolution are freely trans-ferred to philosophy'.[3] But the organic concept of the state was not new: it had a history that stretched back as far as Aristotle, and more recently Burke and Coleridge had brought it into mainstream British political thought. Gladstone, who was indebted both to Aristotle and to Burke, spoke of the state as an organic whole, and he was wholly uninfluenced by the Darwinian revolution. Organic imagery in language about society and the state fed on many sources other than evolutionary biology: on idealist philosophy, for instance, and on the renewal of interest in Greek political thought and the Greek polity. 'Organicism' therefore did not generate a single coherent political theory. Instead, it pervaded the terms of political argument, to such a degree that scarcely any political thinker of note in the late-Victorian and Edwardian period was untouched by its influence.

What were the political implications of organicism? The first point to underline is that while the organic analogy was deployed vigorously by New Liberals such as Hobson and Fabians such as Webb and Shaw, all of whom thought that it vindicated collectivist solutions to social problems, it could also be used to serve quite different political ends. This was part-ly because organicists held a range of different views about whether organic growth was spontaneous or whether it was induced by conscious human contrivance through political action. A good number of late-Victorian anti-collectivists, activists in such pressure groups as the Liberty and Property Defence League, followed Herbert Spencer in giving organicism and evolutionism a conservative twist. These anti-collectivists included the Conservative publicist Lord Hugh Cecil, who seized on the notion that society was like an organism and inferred that it could there-fore not be reordered at will, since it was the result of a process of natural growth. This was a recognizably Burkean argument, and it is illuminat-ing to find Cecil playing a leading role in the retrospective construction of a British Conservative tradition in which, for the first time, Burke fea-tured prominently, for Burke had previously been invoked more fre-quently by Liberals than by Conservatives. Now he was presented as a Conservative precisely because he depicted the social order as an organic growth which could not be reformed mechanically. This suggests an important point: whereas a tension has often been highlighted between the organicist and the free-market capitalist aspects of British conservatism, in fact the two traditions were forged simultaneously and dovetailed neatly. Organicism served as an important weapon for late-Victorian and Edwardian individualists in their struggle against collectivism.

But the weakness of this conservative organicism, as advanced liberals such as Ritchie pointed out, was that it treated the growth of the state as if it somehow stood outside the natural growth of society, rather than forming an integral and 'organic' part of it.[4] Whereas conservatives deployed organicism as a weapon against the interventionist state, radicals tended to use it to counter individualists' resistance to social reform. For if society was akin to an organism, it followed that the individual was a social construct; and if the individual was constituted by society, then phenomena such as pauperism should be treated not as the products of moral failings in the individual, but of structural problems in society. Structural reform through the agency of the state need not necessarily undermine individual self-reliance, but only one particular socially constructed variety of individualism.

Ever since John Burrow's classic study *Evolution and Society* was published in 1966 it has been difficult to sustain the notion that the developmental character of later Victorian thought was attributable to the impact of Darwinism. The nineteenth-century intellect was obsessed with the notion of time, and it became something of a commonplace that any phenomenon had to be understood as part of a long-term process of incremental change. This assumption was shared by such different pre-Darwinian thinkers as J. S. Mill and Gladstone, and it shaped the cultural climate in which Darwin wrote. This is not to belittle Darwin's achievement, nor to deny the challenge he posed to religious orthodoxy. It is to say that he did not so much create as crystallize a conflict between developmentalism and scriptural fundamentalism. His challenge was not intrinsically deeper than that posed by *Essays and Reviews*, a contemporaneous collection of essays in theological revisionism by liberal churchmen. This, just as much as *Origin of Species*, was saturated with developmental assumptions. Similarly, the greatest influence on the Victorian vogue for evolutionary accounts of social institutions was Sir Henry Maine's *Ancient Law*, a work published in 1861 but conceived before Darwin wrote.

The most famous Victorian social evolutionist was the philosopher Herbert Spencer (1820–1903). Spencer coined the phrase 'the survival of the fittest' which has come to encapsulate Darwinism, but he was by no means a straightforward follower of Darwin, and the key elements of his evolutionism had taken shape before the publication of *Origin of Species*. Spencer would have encountered a loose kind of evolutionary outlook in the provincial dissenting circles in which he was brought up, and he acquired an interest in Lamarck's theory of evolution in 1840 when he read Lyell's *Principles of Geology*, which expounded Lamarck's theory of evolution in order to refute it. Spencer, however, was more impressed by the theory itself than by its refutation. In an embryonic form evolutionary ideas were present in his early expositions of his radical *laissez-faire* liberalism. But it was in the early 1850s – years before Darwin wrote – that Spencer came to see the phenomenon of evolution as the key to understanding the universe. His aim was henceforth 'to set forth a general theory of Evolution as exhibited throughout all orders of existences'.[5]

Spencer was first and foremost an evolutionist, and his organicism, far from enjoying equal status, was dependent upon and subordinate to his evolutionism. It might seem strange to insist on this point, for it is obvious that these two doctrines were intimately related elements in late nineteenth-century social thought. If society was like an organism, it would be subject to a process of evolutionary development; and conversely, if society was the product of evolutionary growth, the implication was that it could not be treated as a human contrivance to be reordered at will. Nevertheless we can draw an analytical distinction between the two doctrines. Spencer did not believe in the hegemony of the biological over the social sciences, and in his evolutionism he did not set out to generalize a specifically biological theory, for his theory did not rest on the premise of an identity between biological and social organisms. His critics, especially advanced Liberals and Fabians, commonly accused him of inconsistency in failing to pursue the logic of the organic analogy: in particular, these critics wanted Spencer to acknowledge that the state was to society what the brain was to the body. But in fact Spencer's position was much more tenable than these critics recognized.[6] He always denied that the social organism possesses a consciousness, a will and purpose of its own. In the classic essay 'The social organism' he recognized that the most important difference between a biological organism and a social organism was that in the former a special tissue alone – rather than each member – is endowed with feeling; and that in the former but not in the latter 'the whole has a corporate consciousness capable of happiness or misery'.[7] Indeed, in *Principles of Sociology* he went still further, and offered 'an emphatic repudiation of the belief that there is any special analogy between the social organism and the human organism'; instead he insisted that 'community in the fundamental principles of organization is . . . the only community asserted'.[8] Spencer's organicism was *structural*: the sign of the organic character of society was not its possession of a collective 'brain', but the fact that the evolution of society followed what he called the 'law of organic progress', namely 'the transformation of the homogeneous into the heterogeneous'.[9] In both the biological organism and the social organism, evolution produces increasing specialization of structure and function. Or, to quote a famously obscure but nevertheless revealing passage from *First Principles*, 'evolution is definable as a change from an incoherent homogeneity to a coherent heterogeneity, accompanying the dissipation of motion and the integration of matter'.

Spencer connected this conception of evolution with his theory of history, according to which social progress consisted in a movement from 'militancy' to 'industrialism'. Here he echoed a host of nineteenth-century European social thinkers, including the Frenchmen Constant and Saint-Simon. A type of society founded on governmental or coercive cooperation, directed towards collective goals such as the waging of war, was supplanted by a type of society founded on spontaneous cooperation, which had as its goal the welfare of individuals. This transition from a primitive, simple, and undifferentiated 'militant' society towards a complex and differentiated 'industrial' society was accompanied by a reduction in the role of the state, for one of the characteristic features of the evolution of organisms was the growing specialization of organs. Far from becoming more extensive, as the analogy between the state and the brain might suggest, the state's functions were becoming ever more strictly confined to those functions which belonged distinctively to it, above all the enforcement of justice. Thus whereas in primitive society there was no clear distinction between religious and political activity and temporal rulers were regarded as gods, industrial societies were characterized by the increasing separation of church and state, of temporal and spiritual domains. Likewise the ever clearer separation of the state from economic activity was a characteristic mark of social progress. So too, as we shall see, was a sharper demarcation between the functions of the state and those of the family: each had a corresponding and distinct system of ethics.

This theory of history, and the associated distinction between societies founded on 'compulsory cooperation' and those founded on 'voluntary association', underpinned Spencer's argument in his famous anti-collectivist polemic *The Man versus the State* (1884). This tract was written in response to the legislative work of Gladstone's second administration (1880–5), which Spencer thought had betrayed the sacred liberal principle of freedom of contract; and it came to serve as the bible of late-Victorian 'individualists'. Spencer maintained that the Liberals of his day had forgotten that, historically, the essence of liberalism had been support for the advent of a society of freely cooperating individuals, as opposed to Toryism, which had historically stood for the maintenance of status-bound society. It is sometimes argued that in this work Spencer's polemical enthusiasm overwhelmed his evolutionary and organicist principles and led him back to the older doctrine of natural rights. But the text does not support this reading. The underlying logic was firmly evolutionary in the sense that Spencer's argument took it for granted that it was absurd to work against the grain of social evolution. Freedom of contract was good because it stood at the basis of the modern social order, which rested on the voluntary cooperation of free individuals. Socialism, by contrast, was a kind of political atavism. Social progress must take the form of a movement from status to contract, because a contrary movement would not correspond with the law of progress, which hinged on the growth of heterogeneity.

Spencer did not believe, however, that the movement from 'militancy' to 'industrialism' was a linear movement, and neither did he believe that it was by any means complete by his own day. In certain circumstances a largely industrial society could revert to militant forms, as Spencer sensed was occurring towards the end of his life. Evolution was determined only in the very long run, and so it implied no 'uniform ascent from lower to higher'. Societies regress as well as progress, and only in the long term was the ascendancy of the superior type – 'the survival of the fittest' – guaranteed. This account of evolution had a two-fold merit. On the one hand it vindicated Spencer's lifelong preference for a market economy and a reduction in the scope of the state's action. But on the other hand, because the triumph of the liberal order was guaranteed only in the long run, and certainly not for the present generation, it legitimized Spencer's passionate engagement in contemporary debates on the rival claims of individualism and collectivism.

Evolutionary assumptions could, however, be used to sustain radically different conclusions from Spencer's. Perhaps the classic Victorian attempt to deploy them for socialist ends was Sidney Webb's contribution to *Fabian Essays* (1889). Webb began by asserting what had by this time become truisms of social and political thought: that 'we can no longer think of the ideal society as an unchanging State', and that 'the necessity of the constant growth and development of the social organism has become axiomatic'. But whereas Spencer identified the decisive long-term social change as the movement from homogeneity to heterogeneity, Webb followed Tocqueville (perhaps an unlikely master) in focusing on 'the irresistible progress of Democracy'. This entailed, not merely 'the substitution of one kind of political machinery for another', as Maine and Spencer thought, but 'a complete dissolution of the nexus by which society was held together under the old régime'. For Webb, the classical liberal era had been an era of transition – or 'period of anarchy' – which had completed the dissolution of the old nexus but failed to forge a new one. It would be brought to an end by a 'new synthesis' grounded in the (re)discovery 'that a society is something more than an aggregate of so many individual units – that it possesses existence distinguishable from those of any of its components'. This 'new scientific conception of the Social Organism' would 'put completely out of countenance the cherished principles of the Political Economist and the Philosophic Radical'.[10]

The contrast between Spencer and Webb is instructive, for it casts light on why organico-evolutionary social thought could generate radically different political prescriptions. For Spencer, as we have seen, it was evolutionism that did most of the work. Because the classical liberal order seemed to accord with a general theory of evolution or organic progress, it followed that it was properly 'organic' in the relevant sense. Webb deployed a stronger concept of the social organism: one which pushed the analogy with the biological organism much further, and so did more work in political argument. To say that society was an organism was to assert the priority of collective organization over the individual's right of self-determination. 'Individualism' was by definition inorganic, and Webb had little difficulty in concluding, as Comte had done before him, that classical liberalism therefore possessed no constructive capacity to create a new kind of society, and therefore did not constitute a new evolutionary form. It was an anarchic interlude, to be brought to a close by the rise of socialism. In a sense, then, Webb derived the direction and content of evolutionary progress from the requirements of organicism.

Evolution and Ethics

In the early part of the nineteenth century intellectuals' quest for system sprang above all from a sense of the disorganizing impact of the 'dual

revolution', industrial and political. By the 1870s intellectual anxiety
had shifted, and now focused on the advent of mass democracy and
on the crisis of faith precipitated by Darwinism and biblical criticism.
Typical of the concerns of the age was the Metaphysical Society, which
following its foundation in 1869 became for a time a major forum for
intellectual debate and embraced among its members the most celebrated intellectual figures of the era. The society had as its chief purpose
to find a unifying core underlying the bewildering variety of doctrines
and intellectual movements of the day. It failed. But it was a historically
illuminating failure, for it demonstrated just how widespread was the
conviction among Victorian intellectuals that they had an urgent
social vocation: to work to the construction of a new intellectual synthesis which would be capable of commanding authority. One of its members, Seeley, defined 'the special characteristic of our age': 'unusual
moral earnestness is combined with an unprecedented perplexity and
uncertainty, [and] the old organs of spiritual life are in a great degree
paralysed at the very moment when spiritual life itself is most active'.[11]

It is against this background that we should understand the late-
Victorian vogue for an evolutionary science of ethics founded on a natural history of morals. It has been observed that this was the first period
in which there had been any systematic study of the history of ethics.[12]
A forerunner of the genre was Lecky's *History of European Morals* (1869);
but the fashion accelerated in later decades, with the publication of such
works as Sidgwick's *Outlines of the History of Ethics for English Readers* (first
published in the *Encyclopaedia Britannica* in 1878), the unitarian James
Martineau's *Types of Ethical Theory* (1885), L. A. Selby-Bigge's *British
Moralists* (1897), and Leslie Stephen's *The English Utilitarians* (1900). The
point to grasp is that this vogue is not to be explained by a disinterested
historical quest, but has to be understood as an integral part of the quest
to place ethics on a 'scientific' basis. The assumption was that ethical values, like natural phenomena, had to be understood as part of a process
of development or 'evolution'; and if understood in that way, conflicts of
values could ultimately be made to dissolve. The disjunction between
fact and value could be overcome.

In European terms, the aspiration to construct a scientific or 'positive'
ethical system is most closely associated with Auguste Comte and his followers, and it is significant that a good number of British Comtists came
from Arnoldian backgrounds. The most notable was the founder of British positivism, Richard Congreve, who had been a favourite pupil of
Dr Arnold's at Rugby in the 1830s. Liberal Anglicans such as Frederick

Temple, Arthur Hugh Clough and Benjamin Jowett, not to mention Arnold himself, were among the earliest students of Comte's works at Oxford. Broad Churchmen and positivists shared the conviction that theirs was an age of transition, wanting consensus: in the word of one prominent positivist, John Morley, the age was 'characteristically and cardinally an epoch in transition in the very foundations of belief and conduct'.[13] Both groups shared the conviction that the urgent need of the time was to identify a new source of moral and social authority.

The historian of ideas Leslie Stephen, first editor of the *Dictionary of National Biography*, was never a positivist in the strict sense. But he was one of the most enthusiastic Victorian advocates of an evolutionary science of morals, and deserves to be considered in this context. The main theme of his literary work, pursued even in the *DNB*, was his quest for an evolutionary science of ethics which could furnish moral certainty and thus overcome an age of cultural crisis. The age he lived in was, he wrote, 'a historical critical one, which had yet to produce original thought of its own, and even despaired of constructive system-building'; and he turned to the history of ideas in the belief that history written from a developmental point of view would explain not only the course of progress, but also the elements that had delayed the emergence of a modern synthetic age. Historical inquiry was thus doubly central to the work of construction.

Though Stephen was never a follower of Comte, he is to be identified as a positivist in the broader sense in that he was persuaded that it was on scientific authority that a modern moral and social order must be founded. In order to understand this conviction we need to grasp what Stephen saw as 'the underlying law of development' whose operation constituted a guarantee of progress. That law, 'the gradual adaptation of the race to its environment', entailed 'a growing conformity between the world of thought and the world of facts'. Scientific knowledge was the source of authority in the modern world because such knowledge, by facilitating the conscious adaptation of the race to its environment, gave power. 'The race which knows most of the physical laws, and can apply them most effectively, has an advantage in that struggle for existence which is not the less keen because its character is concealed among civilised races.'[14]

This was a Lamarckian model of historical development: societies which prospered did so not as the result of the workings of a process akin to natural selection – whereby societies which were less 'fit' were eliminated – but because of a process of conscious adaptation to the environment and the acquisition of characteristics which could be transmitted to future generations. This 'scientific' perspective could easily be yoked to a Burkean reverence for institutions and customs that had survived and evolved over generations, for Stephen understood the Burkean notion of prescription precisely in the light of the process of adaptation to the environment. It was a vehicle for the inheritance of the acquired characteristics of a society by successive generations.[15]

In the light of the preceding discussion it is hardly surprising that the work Stephen considered to be his most important contribution to the thought of his age was *The Science of Ethics* (1882), even though its critical reception was unfavourable. In this work he set about transforming ethics into an evolutionary science, one which must begin not with the individual but with society considered as an organism. He explored the ways in which certain types of moral sentiment corresponded to certain types of society. Stephen believed that his science of ethics could transcend the conflict between utilitarians and intuitionists. Both were right in certain respects, he believed: utilitarians in saying that the moral law was external and capable of being derived empirically, and the intuitionists in saying that it was internal. According to Stephen, the moral law was external in being grounded in a relationship between the social tissue and the environment, but it became internal as the individual internalized instinct and feelings generated by that relationship. Furthermore, the utilitarians were right to see a connection between pleasure and moral behaviour, but it was not the case that pleasure and pain constituted the criteria for judging moral conduct. Rather, morally good behaviour would normally be pleasurable just because it constituted an efficient adaptation to the environment; but individuals might perform painful actions as the outcome of internalized virtues or social instincts whose object was indeed the good of the race.[16]

Stephen's projected 'science of ethics' may be contrasted with the sceptical outlook of Darwin's disciple T. H. Huxley, who in his famous Romanes lecture at Oxford in 1893 argued against the notion that fitness in the evolutionary sense constituted moral goodness. 'Social progress', he wrote, 'means a checking of the cosmic process at every step and the substitution for it of another, which may be called the ethical process: the end of which is not the survival of those who happen to be the fittest in respect of the whole of the conditions which obtain, but of those who are ethically the best.'[17] Whereas Stephen identified morality with the dictates of evolution, so that conscience could be defined as 'the utterance of the public spirit of the race, ordering us to obey the primary conditions of its welfare',[18] Huxley asserted that 'if there is one thing plainer than another, it is that neither the pleasures nor the pains of life, in the merely animal world, are distributed according to desert';[19] so that 'the ethical progress of society depends, not on imitating the cosmic process, still less in running away from it, but in combating it'.[20]

The importance of Huxley's lecture was twofold. Coming as it did from the foremost publicist of Darwinism, it disappointed many who hoped to find in the biological sciences the foundation for an authoritative understanding of the social organism. But it also converged with the concerns of a myriad of late-Victorian social thinkers who, attracted as they might be by the imagery of organicism, were persuaded that the fundamental problems of the age were ethical ones which could not be reduced to biology.

It is against the background of the work of Leslie Stephen, Huxley and others that we should consider the work of the most famous proponent of Social Darwinism of the late-Victorian period, Benjamin Kidd. Kidd's best-known work, *Social Evolution* (1894), was published in wake of Huxley's Romanes lecture, and Kidd deliberately set out to respond to the argument that evolutionary science was not equipped to solve or eliminate the ethical problem. He thought that Huxley exemplified 'the negative and helpless position of science', unable to decide between state socialism and *laissez-faire*, and unable to say clearly whether 'science' supported the claims of the one or the other. 'There is at the present time no science of human society', Kidd lamented, for 'science' had 'no clear perception of the nature of the social evolution we are undergoing'.[21] The result was that 'change, transition, and uncertainty' characterized 'those departments of knowledge which deal with social affairs'.[22] Kidd's book, he told an interviewer, was an attempt 'to give a biological basis to our social science'.[23]

Kidd shared some characteristic beliefs of conservative Social Darwinists, notably as regards the inevitability and evolutionary desirability of competition. These beliefs owed much to the German zoologist August Weismann, who sought to purge zoology of the residue of Lamarckism. For Weismann, natural selection was the sole cause of evolution, and it worked through heritable variations resulting from changes in genetic particles.[24] But though these ideas might easily be put to conservative and élitist uses, on policy matters Kidd had more in common with New Liberals and Fabians.[25] He envisaged 'the progressive extension of [the state's] sphere of action to almost every department of our social life'.[26] He was careful to insist that what he was advocating was not socialism, for that was a doctrine which aimed to suspend that rivalry and competition without which there would be no progress. Instead, Kidd wanted the state to take responsibility for placing the competitive struggle on a basis of real equality by means of the '*social* enfranchisement' of the masses to complement their political enfranchisement. The result would be that 'the rivalry of life' would not only be fairer but also, much more importantly, more competitive.

Kidd's most original and interesting contribution to political thought was perhaps his discussion of the problem of inter-generational distributive justice and the way it impinged on the feasibility of reconciling a progressive social science with democratic institutions and the 'interest philosophy'. He took it for granted that the socialist programme was patently antagonistic to the prospect of the continuing progress of the social organism, and hence to the interests of future generations; but he could see no rational argument to persuade today's workers to abstain from present enjoyment out of deference to the interests of others yet to be born.[27] The key problem was that progress depended upon conditions (such as the unequal distribution of resources) which 'have not any sanction from [man's] reason' (reason being interpreted in a narrowly utilitarian sense) and which 'have had no such sanction at any stage of his history'. He asserted the 'fundamental principle' that in the 'social development which has been in progress throughout history, and which is proceeding with accelerated pace in our modern civilisation ... the interests of the individual and those of the social organism to which he belongs are not identical'.[28]

Religion provided Kidd with his solution. He maintained that scientists, including most early sociologists, had been blinded by their antagonism towards religion and had failed to see the evolutionary function of religious beliefs. This function was, he argued, 'to provide a *super-rational* sanction for that large class of conduct in the individual, necessary to the maintenance of the development which is proceeding, but for which there can never be, in the nature of things, any *rational* sanction'. The project of constructing a *rational religion* must be counted chimerical, for 'the essential element in all religious beliefs must apparently be the *ultra*-rational sanction which they provide for social conduct'.[29]

Stephen, Huxley and Kidd were all, in different ways, followers of Darwin: all believed that Darwin's work constituted a fundamental revolution in the world of ideas. They came to very different conclusions about whether science made religion redundant, and whether an understanding of social evolution could generate solid ethical principles; but all were in their different ways absorbed by the ethical problem. None had much sympathy with the more extreme brands of Social Darwinism propounded by, for example, Darwin's cousin the eugenicist Sir Francis Galton, who was prepared to countenance 'stern compulsion' in order to limit the breeding of those he deemed dysgenic undesirables. To Kidd's horror, Galton maintained that 'we must leave morals as far as possible out of the discussion, not entangling ourselves with the almost hopeless difficulties they raise as to whether a character as a whole is good or bad'.[30] In his Herbert Spencer Lecture at Oxford in 1907 he argued for 'interference with the pitiless course of Nature' to improve the racial qualities of mankind. Only nationally desirable physical and mental qualities should be allowed to be reproduced.

Idealism and Society

In some ways the late-Victorian discovery of 'society' owed less to organicism than to philosophical idealism, which flourished from the 1870s onwards under the influence of T. H. Green and his Oxford disciples. Indeed, it is now coming to be appreciated just how much the idealists contributed, not only to the revival of formal political theory, but also to the project of a science of society.[31] Until quite recently this would have been thought a paradoxical assertion, for it was supposed that idealism was something of an alien presence in British intellectual history, and that it stood in antagonism to the largely positivist project of forging a social science. The positivists were concerned with science, the idealists with ethics, and there was little common ground between them. Yet a number of prominent idealists – D. G. Ritchie and Samuel Alexander, for example – were engaged on a projected synthesis of idealist philosophy and evolutionary science; while another prominent idealist, Bernard Bosanquet, displayed a deep interest in the work of continental sociologists such as Durkheim. The whole tendency of late-Victorian social thought was to yoke 'science' and 'ethics' together, and the idealists shared this interest to the full.

Certainly there is little justification for the notion that idealism was an alien presence in British intellectual history. It would be truer to say that the idealists were concerned with giving a sounder philosophical foundation to some of the central tenets of high Victorian liberalism. As we have seen, Mill had implicitly rejected the concept of the 'unencumbered self' as the foundation for liberal doctrine. An adequate account of liberty must rest on an account of the human good. The idealists built on this insight and articulated it much more explicitly than Mill had done. They also gave a more substantive account of the nature of that good.

Idealism also drew on the Liberal Anglican tradition: on the idea of the ethical state, on the critique of the 'negative' concept of liberty, and on the identification of nationality as the key principle that sustained men's attachment to the common good. Indeed, the emergence of idealism could largely be explained in religious terms. After all, the influence of 'external' forces such as the discovery of German idealism and the rediscovery of Hellenic political theory can hardly be understood without some sort of internal account of why these influences should have had some leverage at that particular moment. By far the most important factor in the rise of idealism in late-Victorian Britain was its ability to formulate a response to the intellectual challenge posed by developmentalism and biblical criticism to orthodox Christianity. A strikingly large number of British idealists were sons of clergy, and idealism furnished an idiom in which the late Victorians could pursue the goal of creating either a modernist reformulation of Christian doctrine or an ethical substitute for it. 'All the pregnant concepts of the modern theory of the state', it has been said, 'are secularized theological concepts.'[32]

The influence of the Arnoldian tradition is unmistakable in the work of T. H. Green, the acknowledged leader of British idealism and, with Bosanquet, its leading political theorist. Green was educated at Rugby under Dr Arnold's successor, Tait, and then at Balliol, where his tutor, Jowett, was at the centre of Arnoldite circles in Oxford. Jowett himself was not a systematic thinker, but his synthesis of Liberal Anglican ideas with Platonism and German idealism was enormously influential on Green and his generation. He belonged to that important strain in British social thought – linking Coleridge, Carlyle and the Arnolds – which cherished state power as an antidote to the excesses of commercialism, selfishness and narrow-minded individualism. The function of the state was not just to prevent disorder but to act as an agent of social and moral progress. The true statesman's thoughts, he wrote in his introduction to Plato's *Gorgias*, 'are fixed not on power or riches or extension of territory, but on an ideal state, in which all the citizens have an equal chance of health and life, and the highest education is within the reach of all, and the moral and intellectual qualities of every individual are freely developed, and the "idea of the good" is the animating principle of the whole'.

Green was the first layman to hold a Balliol fellowship, and he was a man of heterodox religious opinions whose decision not to take holy orders was quite deliberate. But like many European secular intellectuals of the period – Ernest Renan is another – he was a deeply spiritual thinker, and the religious inspiration of his political thought is clear. His theological ideas, as expounded in his lay sermons, were to have a profound impact on the religious thought of the late Victorian age. R. W. Macan, Master of University College, described Green in 1917 as 'a master mind in our spiritual building' and 'a missionary of the spirit'.

The religious origins of British idealism may be traced in part to Hegel's critique of the conception of God as self-sufficient and transcendent. This conception, according to Hegel, was irreconcilable with the act of creation, for God requires nature for his own self-completion and thus achieves his self-realization in creation and in human history. On the basis of this concept of the immanence of God, the British idealists were able to argue for a wider understanding of the concept of the incarnation: the person of Jesus, God and Man, was a symbol of the continuing self-revelation of God in history and human institutions. This was the theological groundwork for a rational, undogmatic and socially committed form of Christianity.

But the significance of the political thought of the British idealists is misunderstood when conceived primarily in terms of the importation of German metaphysics for the purpose of combating native intellectual traditions. It would be truer to say that they gave a new philosophical foundation to ideas which were commonplace to mid-nineteenth-century Liberal Anglicans. Green himself owed heavy debts to Carlyle, from whom his critique of the negative concept of liberty was largely derived, and to F. D. Maurice.

The pivot of Maurice's theology, as we have seen, lay in his conviction that God is made known to humanity through his creation, and that the divine is to be identified in imperfect human institutions like family and nation. The idealists built on this conviction and held that actual human communities such as families and states stood as sacramental signs of the divine. These communities sustained the moral life, and in doing so diminished the harsh opposition between self-interest and obligation to others. This was the foundation of Green's most famous work of political theory, the *Lectures on the Principles of Political Obligation* (1879). There he maintained that the basis of the state was not force, not 'the presence of a supreme or independent coercive power, to which habitual obedience is rendered by a certain multitude of people'. That was simply 'the outward visible sign of a state'. The state, according to Green, was a moral organism, and not a purely natural entity. It exists for the promotion of the common good, and the individual feels bound to it 'by ties analogous to those which bind him to his family, ties derived from a common dwelling-place with its associations, from common memories, traditions and customs, and from the common ways of feeling and thinking which a common language and still more a common literature embodies'.[33] This sharp distinction between moral and natural organisms was fundamental to the divergence of idealism from evolutionism.

Green's attachment to the national principle, as the most important of the bonds that tied men to the common good, was derived not only from Maurice but also from the Italian patriot Mazzini, whom Green along with many of his progressive contemporaries venerated. He deplored the reduction of national sentiment to 'the desire for one's own nation to show more military strength than others'. Instead he argued, in Mauricean terms, that the vindication of national sentiment was to be found in the principle that 'the love of mankind . . . needs to be particularised in order to have any power over life and action'.[34]

At the heart of idealist political theory was a critique of the atomistic individualism that they attributed to the utilitarian tradition. Society was no mere aggregate of individuals, but was 'organic', though not in a naturalistic sense: the key point was that society was endowed with a moral purpose, and that the individual acquired a moral purpose through membership of a complex institutions. It was in that sense that society was prior to the individual. Unlike the pluralists of the early twentieth century, who shared their sense of the primacy of social groups over the individual, the idealists attributed primacy to the state, which was not just one social institution among many, but enjoyed a transcendent standing. Green and his fellow idealists built on Liberal Anglican foundations in converting Victorian liberalism to a more positive view of the state as an agent for the realization of 'true freedom', which Green defined, crucially, in moral terms, as 'a positive power or capacity of doing or enjoying something worth doing or enjoying'.[35]

The spiritual and social reformist dimensions of late-Victorian idealism were both evident, too, in Arnold Toynbee, a pupil of Green's at Balliol whose posthumous *Lectures on the Industrial Revolution of the Eighteenth Century in England* (1884) did much to shape the emergent discipline of economic history and to yoke it to a commitment to social reform and a critique of classical economics. Toynbee and his followers considered themselves socialists; but theirs was a socialism, like Maurice's, rooted not in historical materialism but in a spiritual quest. 'The end and law of progress', he wrote, 'is the unity of the human spirit.'

Toynbee shared the Liberal Anglican belief in the critical importance of infusing the state with religious values. 'The State divorced from religion becomes *Antichrist* in reality. All the most powerful emotions of society are enlisted against it.' He wanted to institute what he termed 'a *divine* democracy'.[36] In characteristically Broad Church fashion, he argued that 'the connection of religion with the State is the most effective check to sacerdotalism in all its different forms, and sacerdotalism is the form of religion which can become fundamentally dangerous to the State'. 'Divine truth', he insisted, was 'the common heritage of mankind' and must be guarded from becoming the possession of a sectarian priesthood. The state alone was capable of securing 'this purer religion whose bond shall be, not rigid dogmas, but worship and prayer, union in liturgy not in articles, whose sole object shall be the spiritualisation of life'.[37]

Like Thomas Arnold, Toynbee was an enthusiastic church reformer, the keynote of his ecclesiological thought being his keen advocacy of lay participation in church government, a theme adumbrated by Arnold in *Principles of Church Reform*.[38] But he was equally committed to the state connection as a guarantee of theological liberalism and hence of the inclusiveness of the national church. This too was a widely shared idealist commitment. Green, for all his heterodoxy, opposed the disestablishment of the Church of England because he thought it would both 'de-moralize' the state and 'denationalize' the clergy. The clergyman would become 'a mere priest or a mere preacher, instead of the leader in useful social work and in the administration of such public business as is not directly administered by the state'. Like the Liberal Anglicans and the Christian Socialists, the idealists resisted the 'subtle tendency to divide the secular and the sacred'. All things were sacred, or at least capable of being sacralized.

Though some, like Toynbee, defined themselves as socialists, few idealists were unqualified advocates of state intervention in economic affairs, and the reason was that they were for the most part highly conscious of the organic character of society, which could not be simply manipulated at will as if it were a mechanism. In particular, the idealists were deeply sensitive to the moral texture of society, to ethical relations between citizens, and to the danger that 'mechanical' intervention might undermine 'character'. For Green, 'it is the business of the state, not indeed directly to promote moral goodness, for that, from the very nature of moral goodness, it cannot do, but to maintain the conditions without which a free exercise of the human faculties is impossible'.[39] The most famous idealist philosopher of the generation after Green was Bernard Bosanquet; and he and his wife Helen (née Dendy), as prominent members of the Charity Organization Society, were tenacious opponents of the Fabian concepts of the administrative state – though they were equally staunch critics of the abstraction of rational economic man.

Specifically, Bosanquet argued in his most famous work, *The Philosophical Theory of the State*, that although the state's ultimate aim was 'the realisation of the best life', nevertheless the state's action should properly be confined to 'hindering the hindrances' to that best life.[40] Government might, for instance, acknowledge illiteracy to be a definite hindrance to the good life, and therefore seek to eliminate it forcibly by means of compulsory education. But it did not follow that the state should take measures which would *directly* conduce to the best life. The reason was that an action performed under compulsion lacked the moral significance of 'an action which arises out of the permanent purposes of a life'. In other words, 'the promotion of morality by force . . . is an absolute contradiction'. All state action, to the extent that it entailed either taxation or else prohibition of a certain kind of behaviour, must necessarily involve the replacement of 'intelligent volition' with 'automatism', and therefore tended to lower the moral character of the citizens. State action could therefore be justified only if it 'liberates resources of character and intelligence greater beyond all question than the encroachment which it involves'.[41] There would have to be clear evidence that the hindrance to be removed was an actual rather than merely potential obstacle to the good life.

The idealists never succeeded in making inroads in Cambridge, where Henry Sidgwick set his face against the new doctrine, and in his *Methods of Ethics* (1874) and later works sought to defend a non-egoistic version of utilitarianism. But in Oxford the idealists held the field, partly because of the extraordinary personal ascendancy enjoyed by Green, and from this bastion idealism exercised a far-reaching influence on national life. This influence touched the orthodox and the heterodox alike. High Churchmen such as Henry Scott Holland, Canon of St Paul's, and Charles Gore, successively bishop of Birmingham and Oxford, set out to synthesize idealism with a deeply corporate and socially conscious Christianity. Both had come under Green's sway at Balliol, but they were also able to draw on existing traditions of incarnational thought developed by such thinkers as Maurice. They helped to found the Christian Social Union, and through it voiced a new brand of Christian Socialism, which – like the earlier brand – was actually an offshoot of liberalism; indeed, its influence on advanced liberalism has rarely been properly appreciated. But idealism also had a deep impact upon those ethical rationalists – such as the conservative Mary Arnold (Mrs Humphry Ward), granddaughter of the patriarch of Liberal Anglicanism – who sought a secular substitute for organized religion and found it in the service of humanity. This was the outlook that helped sustain the settlement movement which had such a formative influence on educated young men and women of the period. It also infused the Ethical Society movement that flourished at the close of the nineteenth century.

It would be misleading to depict late-Victorian idealism simply as a philosophical foundation for a more collectivist version of liberalism. This would be to distort the complex relationship between theoretical systems and practical stances. After all, while T. H. Green was an advanced liberal, and was impatient with J. S. Mill's liberalism because he found it a hindrance to the development of a 'new' liberalism, the leading 'new liberal' theorist of the Edwardian generation, L. T. Hobhouse, was a life-long antagonist of philosophical idealism: unable to accept the idealists' emphasis on harmony, he saw conflict as the more usual condition of society. He was more eager to embrace Mill's legacy than to repudiate it. J. A. Hobson, in *The Crisis of Liberalism*, classed idealism as one of 'the tactics of Conservatism',[42] and he based his organicism on biology rather than on philosophy. Meanwhile, two of the most prominent idealist philosophers of this generation, F. H. Bradley and Bernard Bosanquet, were more or less conservative in their social and political attitudes, although Bosanquet considered himself a liberal of a rather advanced kind. Interestingly, Bosanquet was critical of Mill's liberty principle not so much because it would 'curtail unduly the province of social interference', but because 'it would leave an easy opening for a transition from administrative nihilism to administrative absolutism; and some such transition seems to have taken place in Mill's later views'.[43] Like other discourses examined in this book, idealism was not a tool at the disposal of one political movement or another, but an arena within which political battles were fought out.

Gender, the Family and the Moral Life

The point has been made that the idealists, though they built on the Liberal Anglicans' rehabilitation of the state, were no state-worshippers.

Like Rousseau, they held that the state had an absolute moral claim on the individual only to the extent that it sustained the common good. Instead, they were concerned with a much broader rehabilitation of the social sentiment, with an understanding of the whole range of social institutions as part of the divine plan. Thus Bernard Bosanquet – whose language, on casual reading, implies extravagant claims on behalf of the state ('the individual mind writ large') – in fact employed a capacious definition of the state, which he took to include the entire fabric of social institutions, from family to school, from church to university, from workplace to political party, through which the individual was moralized and socialized. It is because so many late-Victorian political thinkers were concerned with the whole nexus of social institutions that it is appropriate to dwell on the most basic of them all, the family. This will also allow us to explore the treatment of gender in Victorian social thought.

There is an influential late twentieth-century feminist critique of nineteenth-century liberalism which rests on two fundamental claims. The generically feminist proposition is that liberalism, understood as a doctrine which accords primacy to individual rights, remained incomplete in the sense that a large category of individuals – married women – were excluded from the enjoyment of rights as individuals, since they were treated in law as their husbands' property. The specifically radical feminist claim goes much further, and argues that this incompleteness was a symptom not so much of the slowness with which liberals realized the full implications of their theory, but rather of a contradiction which lies at the heart of that theory. For the liberal understanding is that freedom rests on a distinction between public and private spheres – the former, that of the state, being conventional, and the latter, that of the family, being natural. And that distinction (so the radical feminist claims) is the foundation of women's subjection, for it identifies the woman's sphere (the sphere of the family, the household, the 'personal') as natural *and therefore* not political. Equal citizenship depends not merely upon equal formal rights such as universal suffrage but also upon substantive equality in the 'private' sphere: hence 'the personal is political'. To circumscribe – as classical liberals did – a private sphere distinct from politics is to perpetuate inegalitarian power relations between the sexes within the family and *therefore* in public life too. The radical feminists, then, 'raise the generally neglected problem of the patriarchal character of liberalism'.[44]

So was Victorian liberalism intrinsically patriarchal? Did it neglect the political importance of the family, treating it as 'natural' and therefore non-political?

To assess the relationship between liberalism and patriarchalism we need to return to John Stuart Mill. For Mill was not just Victorian liberalism's most authoritative and important philosophical exponent; he was also the author of the most influential feminist text published anywhere in the nineteenth century: *The Subjection of Women* (1869). For a long time he was treated as one of the few men with an uncontested place in the feminist canon: that is how he was treated, for instance, in Kate Millett's now classic account.[45] Recently, however, feminists have tried to re-read Mill's book as demonstrating the limitations of liberal feminism. They have argued that Mill's feminism was of a pale and bloodless variety compared with that of his wife Harriet Taylor; and that she, not Mill, deserves to be remembered as the truly radical voice of the time.

This reading of Mill and Taylor rests primarily on a comparison of the paper on the 'Enfranchisement of women' published in the *Westminster Review* in 1851 with the book on *The Subjection of Women*, which was written in 1861, though not published until eight years later. The former, though placed for publication by Mill and assumed by some to be his work, was on his own admission the work of his wife, his own role being 'little more than that of an editor and amanuensis'. The latter, though again the fruit of intellectual collaboration, was composed three years after Harriet Taylor's death. Differences between the two works are therefore taken to be attributable to the differences between Harriet Taylor's feminism and Mill's. The key point emphasized by radical feminist critics is that the two texts take very different views of the relationship between the notion of the egalitarian family and the notion of women's participation in the workforce. In her article on the 'Enfranchisement of women', Taylor argued trenchantly against any concessions to the doctrine of separate spheres. Even if women's participation in the workforce had the effect of diminishing wage and salary levels, it would be better for a given income to be earned jointly by husband and wife rather than by husband alone, since 'a woman who contributes materially to the support of the family, cannot be treated in the same contemptuously tyrannical manner as one who, however she may toil as a domestic drudge, is a dependent on the man for subsistence'.[46] In other words, the relative financial contributions of husband and wife to the household budget were a crucial determinant of domestic power relations. In *The Subjection of Women*, by contrast, Mill's emphasis was different. He agreed that women must be educated for work in the same way as men, for 'the *power* of earning is essential to the dignity of a woman, if

she has not independent property'; but he did not believe that this principle implied the *actual* participation of married women in the workforce, nor the equal distribution of domestic tasks.

> When the support of the family depends, not on property, but on
> earnings, the common arrangement, by which the man earns the income
> and the wife superintends the domestic expenditure, seems to me in
> general the most suitable division of labour between two persons.[47]

Mill's critics – even sympathetic ones – have therefore suggested that,
even though he made some crucial steps towards the transcendence of
'patriarchal liberalism', nevertheless 'his continuing affirmation of a
traditional division of labor within the family, which he shares with his
male liberal predecessors, would on the logic of his own analysis defeat
the sexual equality to which he is committed'.[48]

But is this argument decisive in historical terms? It is arguable that it
overlooks some important points about the contexts in which the two
works were composed and published, and the strategies they employed.
On Mill's own account it was the 1851 article which practically inaugurated the public discussion of the question of the emancipation of
women, whereas by the time *The Subjection of Women* was published, in
1869, the issues of women's suffrage, women's education, and married
women's property rights were very much on the political agenda, due
not least to the efforts of Mill himself as MP for Westminster from 1865
to 1868. And though Mill was self-consciously radical in *The Subjection of
Women*, and deliberately rejected the conciliatory approach, it would
scarcely have been helpful to his cause – as the most celebrated public
figure associated with the cause of women's rights – to yoke his case to an
advocacy of a revolution in gender roles within the household. As it was,
a number of his allies wondered whether he had not chosen to fight on
too broad a front by positively arguing that women did have an aptitude
for public occupations, rather than contenting himself with the proposition that only a genuinely free market could demonstrate whether or
not they had such an aptitude.[49]

There is a second strand in the radical feminist critique of Mill. He
was, as Barbara Caine has observed, notably dismissive of the idea that
women might have a new and distinctive contribution to make to civic
life, one founded on their experience as mothers and as managers of the
household. Mill's whole case consisted in a deconstruction of arguments
about women's 'nature', which he took to be shaped by social institutions;

and he held that it was indeed true that women as they were were patently unsuited to public life, but that this was not because they were naturally unfitted, but because they had lacked exposure to the public world. Caine, somewhat tendentiously, records Mill's 'insistence that men embody the universal standard of human excellence', and concludes that 'his approach demonstrates some of the fundamental problems involved in any attempt to graft feminism on to an unreconstructed liberalism'.[50]

One problem with the account advanced by radical feminist political theorists is that it follows a rather outdated interpretation in exaggerating the conventionalism of Victorian political thought – exaggerating, that is to say, the salience of the belief that the state is (unlike the family) a product of human contrivance. The belief in a sharp distinction between the 'natural' family and the 'artificial' or 'conventional' state is difficult to reconcile with the Hellenic cast of so much Victorian writing about social institutions. For central to that world-view was the belief that the state, just as much as the family, was a 'natural' institution. Conversely, a central tenet of much late-Victorian social theory was that the family was the basic social institution, providing the model for other social institutions, including the state.[51] This idea was fundamental to Sir Henry Maine's classic *Ancient Law*.

Maine's work was directed primarily against contractual theories of the origins of political society, and he sought to show that the individual and the contract stood not at the origin of social development, but as products. This thesis was embedded in an historical-anthropological controversy about the origins of the family. Against Sir John Lubbock and others, Maine propounded the patriarchal theory of the origin of society: the family, founded on the authority of husband and father, provided the model for other social institutions, including the state. His work was therefore welcomed by opponents of individualism, such as Maurice, who saw it as a 'scientific' vindication of their critique of 'independent morality', or the notion of the individual as the prime source of moral worth.[52] Conversely, modern feminist scholars, seizing on the patriarchal theory, have concluded that Maine's argument was essentially a defence of the Victorian system of domestic authority.[53] But in fact its practical significance was double-edged. Maine, after all, was an evolutionist, in the sense that he assigned normative significance to the direction of social change. If his work helped undermine contractual or individualistic accounts of the origin of society, it also identified contractual relations as a pervasive feature of modern and 'progressive' society.

This was the point of his famous dictum 'that the movement of the progressive societies has hitherto been a movement from *Status to Contract*'.
What is not generally recognized is that this dictum was formulated in
the context of a discussion of family law. 'The movement of the progressive societies' – the passage begins, in a preliminary formulation – 'has
been uniform in one respect. Through all its course it has been distinguished by the gradual dissolution of family dependency and the
growth of individual obligation in its place. The Individual is steadily
substituted for the Family, as the unit of which civil laws take account.'
In *Ancient Law* Maine did not construe this dictum to mean that the
woman's subordination to her husband was diminishing. Rather, what
he had in mind was the erosion of her subjection to the authority of her
father, and other male blood-relations. Just as slavery had been super-
seded by the contractual relations of master and servant, so 'the status of the
Female under Tutelage, if the tutelage be understood of persons other
than her husband, has also ceased to exist; from her coming of age to her
marriage all the relations she may form are relations of contract'.[54]

Ancient Law was written before the issue of women's rights was
brought onto the political agenda as the franchise question was raised in
the reform debates in the 1865 parliament. In addition, the publication
of Mill's *Subjection of Women*, and the attempt by Gladstone's first government to deal with the issue of married women's property rights, meant
that the political and intellectual climate had changed by the mid-1870s,
when Maine published his *Lectures on the Early History of Institutions*
(1875). In these lectures Maine followed up themes he had first
addressed in *Ancient Law*; but in the lecture most relevant to our concerns – on 'The early history of the settled property of married women' –
his emphasis was subtly different. He was still concerned with the concept of the patriarchal family, which he defined as consisting 'of animate
and inanimate property, of wife, children, slaves, land, and goods, all
held together by subjection to the despotic authority of the eldest male
of the eldest ascending line, the father, grandfather, or even more
remote ancestor'; and his emphasis was again on its erosion.[55] His thesis
was that Roman law had begun by conceiving of the wife as becoming, by
marriage, the daughter of her husband, all her property thus becoming
his; but by virtue of the emergence of forms of marriage 'without coming
under the hand' of the husband, it came to formulate the principle that
the wife's property should remain under her own control, except when
(as would normally be the case) a part of it was formed into a dowry.
Hindu law stood in direct contrast, for though it possessed a notion of

the settled property of a married woman, it did not develop this institution further, but tended to reduce it it scope. Thus whereas in *Ancient Law* Maine was primarily concerned with the ways in which the originally supreme authority of the father was diminished, in this later lecture he was concerned with the erosion of the authority of the husband.

But the crucial point is the broader significance Maine attached to these developments, and to the contrast between the ways in which Hindu law and Roman law dealt with married women's property. Maine was no enthusiast for the cause of what he termed 'the so-called enfranchisement of women'. But he did not believe sexual inequalities to be *sui generis*. On the contrary, the legal changes he described formed, he thought, 'merely a phase of a process which has affected very many other classes, the substitution of individual human beings for compact groups of human beings as the units of society'. They were, in other words, an aspect of the movement of progressive societies from status to contract. And he recognized that the assimilation of the legal position of women to the legal position of men would be the final stage in completing the process. He was, indeed, prepared to assent to the proposition that 'the degree in which the personal immunity and proprietary capacity of women are recognised in a particular state or community is a test of its degree of advance in civilisation'.[56]

Feminist scholarship has plainly been crucial in highlighting the importance of the family in political and social thought. The late-Victorian discovery of 'society' was coupled with a growing interest in the place of the family in social theory; something which was evident in wider European thought, most notably in the writings of the Frenchman Frédéric Le Play. In this context we might note the importance of the household as the basic unit of late-Victorian social investigation, especially that type of social investigation practised by the Charity Organization Society.

A key work here was Helen Bosanquet's *The Family* (1906). Mrs Bosanquet, wife and collaborator of the idealist philosopher Bernard Bosanquet, began by noting 'how seldom the present student or reformer of society shows any recognition of the importance of the Family as compared with other and more artificial institutions'; but she recognized that this neglect was disappearing, for she commented that 'it is mainly in recent years that the Family as an institution has attracted the attention of the thinker and historian'.[57] But if Mrs Bosanquet saw the family, rather than the individual, as the basic unit of society, this was not to say that she saw the internal organization of the family or household as irrelevant to the state. Far from it. For Helen and Bernard

Bosanquet, public and private were not rigidly demarcated 'separate spheres', but points on a continuum. The importance of the family, as the basic and natural social unit, was that it nurtured altruistic sentiments, and so 'presented itself as the medium by which the public interest is combined with private welfare'. Mrs Bosanquet depicted the life of the family as a sort of microcosm of the civic life of the state, and a school of citizenship:

> The first and essential step towards an enlightened democracy, a people able to rule the nation wisely, and to find their own interests in the common welfare, is a generation of women fit to be the mothers of such a people, and to make the homes in which wisdom and self-control may be the ruling spirits.[58]

Asking why the family should not be swept away as 'a narrow-minded and exclusive organisation' – an obstacle, as Plato taught, to the citizen's primary allegiance to the state – she replied that 'the Family, with its mingled diversity and identity of interests, is the best – if not indeed the only – school for the life of the citizen'.[59]

Helen Bosanquet was by no means a straightforward defender of the institution of the family as it existed in her time. On the contrary, she identified a number of pathological features in family life as she observed it, and notably 'the age-long rivalry between the Family and the State'. Her remedy was precisely the greater involvement of women in the public sphere, for it was the sharp distinction between the sphere of women and the sphere of men that accounted for the pathological condition of the family. The consequence of this dissolution of the separate spheres would be, paradoxically enough, the strengthening of the family as one of those sinews of a healthy social life independent of the state:

> That the Family should exercise a narrowing and selfish influence over its members is inevitable so long as one of the partners responsible for it is excluded from intelligent participation in the work of the State, and sees in public services only rival claims to those of the Family. Get rid of that narrowing and selfish influence and the Family will become to an extent never known before the source and inspiration of noble and enlightened service to the State. And, on the other hand, in proportion as this is true, the State will recognise the infinite importance of the Family and cease from those insidious attacks upon it which arise mainly from ignorance of its true function.[60]

In viewing the family as a microcosm of the state, the Bosanquets were drawing on an important tradition in idealist thought. T. H. Green had taken a radical stance on relations within the family, advocating complete equality between husband and wife in the exercise of authority within the household, and identical (and extensive) rights of divorce.[61] Like J. S. Mill, and like the Bosanquets too, Green saw family life as an ethical training-ground, and a preparation for citizenship: 'The more completely a marriage is "the sharing of an entire life", the more likely are the external conditions of a moral life to be fulfilled in regard both to married persons and their children'. This conception of the family was, significantly, rejected by an old liberal such as Herbert Spencer, who insisted on a rigid distinction between the ethics of the family and the ethics of the state. The ethics of the state were determined by justice, or 'the natural relation of conduct and consequence'. The ethics of the family, by contrast, rested on the very different principle of altruism, and the weaker members were shielded by the stronger from the natural consequences of their conduct. If women were admitted to political life, Spencer feared, the two kinds of ethics might be confused, and the ethics of the family introduced into the state, with disastrous results.[62] It was, appropriately enough, D. G. Ritchie – the Darwinian idealist – who took Spencer to task for these teachings. Like other idealists, Ritchie could not accept this antithesis between the ethics of the family and those of the state, and replied that 'the family ideal of the state', though not easy to attain, was much preferable to 'the policeman theory', because it would entail 'the moralisation of politics'. 'The cultivation of separate sorts of virtues and separate ideals of duty in men and women has led to the whole social fabric being weaker and unhealthier than it need be.'[63]

Late-Victorian and Edwardian feminism – and the wider upsurge of interest in 'the woman question' and the family in social theory – need to be set against the background of the deep ethical bias in the political and social thought of the period; a bias which was actually strengthened in the late-Victorian period. It was something of a stereotype in biological thought that women, if perhaps underendowed with the capacity for abstract reasoning, were specially endowed with moral qualities that fitted them for service to others. Women, wrote Geddes and Thomson in an influential work, had evolved 'a larger and habitual share of the altruistic emotions', and excelled 'in constancy of affection and sympathy'.[64] Notions such as these might be considered tendentious props for reactionary conceptions of 'separate spheres' in which women were called to be mothers, and in which (if they had any public role at all) they were to devote themselves to charitable works in which their powers of sympathy, intuition and attention to detail could be fully employed; they were not, however, to involve themselves in the competitive and hence masculine worlds of business and national politics. But in a cultural context in which differentiation – including differentiation of the sexes – was commonly held to be a source of evolutionary progress, and in which altruism was esteemed, a number of prominent feminists exploited ideas about gender differences for their own purposes. Millicent Fawcett and Frances Power Cobbe both depicted the maternal role as the evolutionary source of 'social sentiment' and 'altruism' in the modern state.[65] Fawcett identified 'the motherhood of women' as 'one of those great facts of everyday life which we must never lose sight of', and insisted that 'we want the home and the domestic side of things to count for more in politics and in the administration of public affairs than they do at present'. And Cobbe defended her anti-vivisectionist activity by arguing that 'if my sex has a "mission" of any kind, it is surely to soften this hard world'.[66]

These were central themes in British social thought. The sort of psychological and moral hedonism which arguably had a tenuous hold even in the age of the so-called utilitarian ascendancy was in full retreat from the 1860s and 1870s onwards. It was supplanted by an ethic of duty and service – whether to God or to some secular substitute like 'Humanity', or to some hybrid of the two. The positivist cult was, famously, a 'Religion of Humanity', and it was Comte himself who coined the term 'altruism' – articulating a scepticism about the notion (which was always more characteristically eighteenth-century than Victorian) that social order might emerge spontaneously from the private interests of individuals. Seeley's *Ecce Homo* – a powerful influence, we have seen, on the Ethical Societies movement – had a chapter entitled 'The Enthusiasm of Humanity', in which humanity was defined as 'neither a love for the whole human race, nor a love for each individual of it, but a love for the race, or for the ideal of man, in each individual'.[67]

It is in the context of the retreat from hedonism towards an ethic of service that we should place Alfred Marshall, the most distinguished economist of his generation and the author of its most authoritative synthesis, his *Principles of Economics* (1890). Marshall's chief significance in the history of economic thought is that he was, in the words of his most distinguished pupil, 'the first great economist *pur sang* that there ever was'.[68] His life was devoted to the construction of economics as a separate science, and to the distress of colleagues such as the philosopher Henry Sidgwick (whom he greatly admired) he succeeded in establishing a separate economics tripos at Cambridge, thus loosing the subject from its moorings in the moral sciences.

Yet there was much more to Marshall than the technical economist. Marshall had come to the study of economics via ethics: as a young Cambridge don in the 1870s he had been engaged in the fashionable quest for an 'ethical creed which is according the the Doctrine of Evolution'.[69] If he was an indefatigable campaigner for the separate identity of the science of economics, it was not that he had ceased to be concerned with ethics. He had decided to pursue the goal of the moralist by other means. Marshallian economics was conceived as a scientific bridge between individualist hedonism and an evolutionary ethical creed. As his professorial successor, A. C. Pigou, put it, 'economics for him was a handmaid to ethics, not an end in itself, but a means to a further end: an instrument, by the perfecting of which it might be possible to better the conditions of human life'.[70] There is an interesting parallel with a Frenchman who was a near contemporary. Emile Durkheim, like Marshall, was deeply concerned with the 'moral problem' – with what happens to notions of duty once religious orthodoxy has been undermined. And just as Marshall pursued the goal of the moralist via the distinct science of economics, so Durkheim devoted his career to proselytizing for the separate discipline of sociology, of which subject he held the first chair in the French university system. But Durkheim's goal, like Marshall's, was ultimately to resolve the moral problem.

Ethics penetrated Marshallian economics primarily through that hegemonic concept in late-Victorian moral and social thought, the idea of character. The classical economists erred, he thought, in regarding man as 'a constant quantity', whereas the new generation of economists appreciated that they had to deal with a science, like biology, whose subject-matter developed over time. Particularly important – as the American social theorist, Talcott Parsons, showed – was Marshall's distinction between wants and activities, a distinction which was effectively introduced right at the beginning of the *Principles*. Only at the earliest stages of social evolution did wants straightforwardly determine economic activities, which were undertaken for the satisfaction of those wants. The further society evolves, the truer it is to say that man's character, and hence his wants, are shaped by his work. 'Man's character',

Marshall wrote on the very first page of the *Principles*, 'has been moulded by his every-day work, and by the material resources which he thereby procures, more than by any other influence unless it be that of his religious ideals.'[71] Even Carlyle would have been tempted to agree.

This perception lay at the heart of Marshall's analysis of poverty, which from his early manhood remained one of his chief practical concerns. The classical economists saw poverty (not pauperism) as the natural condition of the labouring classes; what neither they nor a later generation of individualists saw was that 'the poverty of the poor is the chief cause of that weakness and inefficiency which are the cause of their poverty'. Hence 'they had not the faith, that modern economists have, in the possibility of a vast improvement in the condition of the working classes'.[72] Marshall reiterated the implications of this analysis of poverty in evidence to a number of official inquiries, most notably to the Royal Commission on the Aged Poor in 1893. There he argued that the doctrine that 'grants in aid of wages lower wages' – and do not relieve the poverty of the wage-earner and his family – was true only insofar as the grants in question were not used in such a way as to increase the industrial efficiency of the working class. But 'a tax levied on the well-to-do for the benefit of those whose means are small may be secured from ultimately lowering wages, provided care be taken that the money is spent for the benefit of the rising generation, or if the relief granted by it is accompanied by more stringent sanitary and educational regulations in their interest which might not be otherwise practicable'.[73] Marshall was, however, no collectivist. He thought it urgently necessary to combat poverty, not so much because of the intrinsic material harm done by poverty, but because of its moral consequences; and so he deprecated mechanistic attempts to relieve poverty that would themselves sap the roots of character. It was in this sense that he wrote to Helen Bosanquet, commending her on the publication of *The Strength of the People*, while disagreeing on some particulars:

> I have always held that poverty and pain, disease and death are evils of greatly less importance than they appear except in so far as they lead to weakness of life and character; and that true philanthropy aims at increasing strength more than at the direct and immediate relief of poverty.[74]

It is plain that Marshall was deeply influenced by evolutionary ideas. He was also fascinated by eugenics, and became a foundation life member of the Cambridge Eugenics Society in 1911. It is fashionable to emphasize the pessimistic implications of these currents of thought, which in thinkers such as Henry Maudsley generated the spectre of racial degeneration.[75] But Marshall is a notable instance of the optimistic interpretation which was surely more common in Britain, if not elsewhere. For Marshall's somewhat Lamarckian belief in the profound impact of the environment upon character combined with a conviction that that environment was modifiable by human agency to nourish a rationally grounded faith in the possibility of sustained improvement. In the summer of 1910 he and Keynes entered into controversy with the doyen of eugenicists, Karl Pearson, whose approach was distinguished by an exclusive emphasis upon heredity as opposed to environment. The Galton Laboratory, which Pearson directed, published a study of alcoholism purporting to demonstrate that children's disabilities were related to hereditary defects rather than to parents' drinking habits. The two Cambridge economists, more inclined than Pearson to highlight the importance of acquired habits, criticized the statistical basis of the study.[76]

Central to Marshall's vision of the ethical significance of economics was his success in severing it from the hedonistic psychology and moral individualism with which it had formerly been associated. Economics, as Marshall conceived it, was not to be defined as the study of man insofar as he is motivated by the desire for wealth; rather, it was concerned with 'just that class of motives which are measurable, and therefore are specially amenable to treatment by scientific machinery'.[77] And measurable motives were by no means exclusively selfish ones, a point Marshall drummed home by citing the case of altruism within the family unit. 'For instance, the chief motives of saving capital, of spending money on the education of children, and of buying things for their use, are unselfish: and the actions which are prompted by them occupy a very large place in economics. The reason is that family affection acts with so much uniformity in any given stage of civilization that its effects can be systematically observed, reduced to law and measured.'[78]

The family unit, indeed, played an important part in Marshall's economic analysis, and this was something of a novelty, for the classical economists had treated the rational individual, and not the family, as the basic economic unit. Marshall's shift of emphasis towards considering the family as a unit was tied to his insistence on the importance of investment in human capital, a feature of his thought which we have already identified in his analysis of poverty. 'The most valuable of all capital', he wrote, 'is that invested in human beings; and of that capital the most precious part is the result of the care and influence of the mother, so long as she retains her tender and unselfish instincts, and has not been hardened by the strain and stress of unfeminine work.' The consequence was that 'in estimating the cost of production of efficient labour, we must often take as our unit the family': that is, 'the cost of production of efficient men together with the women who are fitted to make their homes happy, and to bring up their children vigorous in body and mind, truthful and cleanly, gentle and brave'.[79]

Though married to an intellectual woman with whom he collaborated closely in his economic work, Marshall was no feminist. He opposed the admission of women to degrees at Cambridge. But women were crucial to his vision of social progress, not as workers themselves but as nurturers of the labour force of the future. In defining the necessities of life for an unskilled labourer, Marshall included 'sufficient freedom for his wife from other work to enable her to perform her maternal and her household duties'; and he criticized the fiscal illusion that led families to act as though the family income were increased by the whole of what the working mother earned. This was to neglect not just the material services the mother might otherwise have rendered in the home, but also 'her moral influence in educating the children, in keeping the household in harmony and making it possible for her husband to be cheered and soothed in his evenings at home'.[80]

In his memoir of Marshall, the Oxford economist F. Y. Edgeworth recalled the central role to be played by family life in Marshall's 'ideal state'. 'The central figure', wrote Edgeworth, 'would be the wife and mother practising pristine domestic virtues'. Marshall was critical of those like J. S. Mill who played down the differences between the sexes. Seeing men and women as having complementary functions, he 'regarded the family as a cathedral, something more sacred than the component parts'.[81]

Critics of the Ethical Polity

The broadly idealist – but also Hellenic – idea that politics, properly understood, revolved around the realization of the good life for man was so widely shared as to exercise something of a bipartisan cultural hegemony in the late-Victorian period. If it was central to the ideas of advanced Liberals, it was equally important to anti-collectivist Liberals such as the Bosanquets and to Unionists of Mary Ward's stamp. Nevertheless it had its critics, especially among conservatives and individualists who resisted the idealist tendency to dissolve boundaries between ethics and politics, between 'self' and 'government', between private and public, between the role of the family and the role of the state. Indeed, one of the most important divisions in late-Victorian political thought lay precisely here: not in the clash of doctrines, but in the conflict between different styles of political thought. Idealists and their allies set about dissolving conceptual antitheses which, as they saw things, created unnecessary and artificial intellectual and political conundrums: Bosanquet, for example, tried to solve the 'paradox of self-government' by eroding the antithesis of 'self' and 'government'. This approach was opposed by a heterogeneous band of critics whose main point in common was a hard-headed empiricist predilection for clear-minded conceptual distinctions. Spencer was one of the most articulate exponents of this intellectual approach, for he attached a great deal of importance to the principle that 'from the lowest to the highest creatures, intelligence progresses by acts of discrimination'.[82] The whole tendency of his interpretation of evolution as a movement towards differentiation and functional specialization was to reinforce boundaries, not to dissolve them. Indeed, a characteristic quality of Spencer's political writings was his determination to clarify political argument by purging it of confusions arising from a failure to draw distinctions between things that were different in essentials.

An early and distinguished manifestation of this sceptical intellectual style was Sir James Fitzjames Stephen's famous polemic *Liberty, Equality, Fraternity* (1873). This was considered by Sir Ernest Barker to be 'the finest exposition of conservative thought in the latter half of the nineteenth century', though its author continued to regard himself as a liberal. Stephen's book is familiar to political theorists as the most cogent contemporary critique of Mill's *On Liberty*, and it was in that sense that it was rediscovered in the debate on the relationship between law and morals in the 1960s; but its significance is broader than that, and Stephen's targets (in so far as he was aiming at Mill) were as much *Utilitarianism* and *The Subjection of Women* as *On Liberty*. The book is directly relevant to our present concerns in that it contains a sustained denunciation of Mill's feminism (*The Subjection of Women*, Stephen wrote, was 'a work from which I dissent from the first sentence to the last'), and also in that its broader polemical thrust was aimed at what Stephen regarded as the optimism and ethical naïveté of the secular religion of democracy. The catchword 'liberty, equality, fraternity' was, he wrote, 'the creed of a religion', a 'Religion of Humanity' which he defined in a sense broader than the Comtean:

It is one of the commonest beliefs of the day that the human race col-
lectively has before it splendid destinies of various kinds, and that the
road to them is to be found in the removal of all restraints on human
conduct, in the recognition of a substantial equality between all
human creatures, and in fraternity or general love. These doctrines
are in very many cases held as a religious faith.[83]

It is illuminating to find Stephen voicing contempt for Seeley's social
gospel. 'With all its defects', he thought, 'Paley's *Evidences* is worth a cart-
load of *Ecce Homos*.' Seeley's book gave 'the impression of being written
by a sheep in wolf's clothing'.[84]

Stephen's book has been invoked in the twentieth century by those
who deny the positivist separation of law and morals – who insist, therefore, that the criminal law must articulate the moral sense of the community. But the central theme of his book was a rather different one: it
was a critique of the 'religious dogma of liberty', the notion of the service
of humanity, and the associated faith in ethical progress. There were two
main elements in Stephen's critique of progress.

First, he denied the assumption that the progress of society is from
bad to good. His view was 'that the progress has been mixed, partly good
and partly bad'. Progress, in other words, was merely linear development, and had no moral significance. Secondly, he denied the possibility
of formulating scientific laws of history from which it would be possible
to deduce values. Thus, for instance, he questioned some of the infer-
ences which contemporaries were wont to draw from Sir Henry Maine's
work, and particularly the notion that force was diminishing in importance as a social bond. 'All that is proved by the fact that status, to use Sir
Henry Maine's expression, tends to be replaced by contract, is that force
changes its form. Society rests ultimately upon force in these days, just as
much as it did in the wildest and most stormy periods of history.'[85]

Among senior politicians, perhaps the most trenchant critic of commonplace late-Victorian assumptions about the interconnectedness of
politics and morals was the Marquis of Salisbury. 'Opinions upon moral
questions', he wrote, 'are more often the expression of strongly felt
expediency than of careful ethical reasoning; and the opinions so formed
by one generation become the conscientious convictions or the sacred
instincts of the next.'[86] Arguments from abstract right were specious
masks for selfish claims and special pleading. The basis of politics, in
Salisbury's view, was not morality but pragmatic self-interest. In one of
the most classically Augustinian of Victorian pronouncements on politics,

he stressed 'the fallibility of human nature, of the proneness of mankind to shape their conduct by their desires, and to devise afterwards the code of morality necessary to defend it'.[87] He propounded a determinedly 'low' view of the purposes of the state, a view curiously similar to that taken by his ancestral enemies, Whigs such as Bishop Warburton in the eighteenth century and Macaulay in the nineteenth. For Salisbury the state was 'a joint-stock company to all intents and purposes...a combination of a vast number of men for well-defined objects – the preservation of life and property'.[88]

Salisbury was one of a number of late-Victorian thinkers who turned the utilitarian criterion of political right – the greatest happiness of the greatest number – against the faith in the 'improvement of man' with which its eighteenth-century inventors had linked it; and he thus tried to sever the link between politics and morals. Salisbury, however, was an ancestral Tory, whereas this tendency to turn utilitarianism to conservative purposes was more common among disillusioned Liberals, and especially among Liberal Unionists who broke with Gladstone in the 1880s, when the Liberal leader not only came out for Irish Home Rule, but also, in his second government, enacted a series of legislative measures which breached the sacred principle of freedom of contract. The Oxford jurist A. V. Dicey had been an enthusiastic contributor to the advanced Liberal *Essays on Reform* in 1867. But he later became both a prominent theorist of Unionism (in *England's Case against Home Rule*, 1886) and the historian of the demise of Benthamism in political thought and public policy in his *Lectures on the Relation of Law and Public Opinion in England during the Nineteenth Century* (1905).

Late nineteenth-century individualists undoubtedly liked to present themselves as true to the radicalism of the Manchester school. They depicted Chamberlainite radicalism and, later, the New Liberalism as versions of a 'New Toryism' which enacted legislation on behalf of one class rather than being guided by the public good. This line of argument was rhetorically powerful, but it would be a mistake to infer that the individualists were simply unyielding adherents of an older doctrine which had been overtaken by events. In fact they made substantial modifications to utilitarian doctrine, and these modifications all tended to serve conservative purposes. This tendency can be seen in the Cambridge moral philosopher Henry Sidgwick, who was the most profound theorist of moderate anti-collectivism. Sidgwick argued that the utilitarian goal of the greatest happiness of the greatest number demanded a practical respect for certain rules which experience showed to be generally conducive to utility. Among these rules the *laissez-faire* principle featured prominently. *Ad hoc* departures from these rules might in isolated cases be beneficial, but their cumulative effect would be to sap confidence in the rule itself.

Sidgwick is particularly significant in the context of this chapter because he was a tenacious philosophical critic of both evolutionism and idealism. Like many evolutionists and idealists his intellectual career was shaped by the loss of faith that afflicted so many intellectuals who reached adulthood about the time of *Origin of Species* and *Essays and Reviews*. Like them, he was anxious to find a new basis for certainty in ethical matters. But he thought that both evolutionism and idealism ultimately had to have recourse to arbitrary and dogmatic assertion. Instead Sidgwick placed his trust in a reconstructed utilitarianism which was now not the opponent of intuitionism but its ally. Commonsense 'intuitions', he held, were not so much the findings of a distinct moral sense as the distillation of the experience of generations as to what kinds of moral rules and practices tended to promote the general happiness. So Sidgwick – in defiance of the example of his master, Mill – urged the utilitarian to 'repudiate altogether that temper of rebellion against the established morality' as something purely external and conventional, and instead to 'contemplate it with reverence and wonder as a marvellous product of nature, the result of long centuries of growth'. Always averse to the quest for grand systems, and remarkably impervious to the influence of intellectual fashion, Sidgwick aimed to make a more limited contribution to the quest for certainty by clarifying political and moral argument. He defined his aim as 'clearness and precision in our general political conceptions, definiteness and consistency in our fundamental assumptions and methods of reasoning'.[89] So, for example, he reiterated the Benthamite definition of liberty as the absence of external impediments to action – the 'negative' definition which, as he well knew, ruled out the idealist tendency to confuse freedom with the good life in general.[90]

Perhaps the most acute critic of the fashionable project of creating a science of society founded on a law of progress was W. H. Mallock, who was arguably the most important theorist of conservatism in the last decades of the nineteenth century. He was in some ways an English analogue of continental thinkers such as Gustave Le Bon and the Italian élite theorists Pareto and Mosca, though he was more profound than Le Bon and less systematic than Pareto. Mallock wrote voluminously, and on a wide range of subjects, from the distribution of national income to the defence of religious belief against the corrosive impact of science, as well as a number of notable novels; and his strength lay in his destructive powers as a critic rather than in his constructive powers as a systematizer. For that reason it is not always easy to distil a coherent doctrine from his writings, which were excessively concerned with undermining the assumptions of other writers, whether Spencer, Kidd or Sidney Webb. Sometimes he was inclined to contest the applicability of scientific explanation to social phenomena, and to treat the faith in scientific method as one of the superstitions of the age. He argued that conservatives ought not to treat science with 'ostentatious civility', but rather to point out 'the arrogance and effrontery of science, of conclusions said to be demonstrated, which really are no conclusions, of the ignorance, of the absurdity, of the confusion of scientific men'.[91] But at other times he set out to show how a true social science could be forged. He urged the creation of a 'science of character' which would establish 'a permanent relationship' between human character and social inequality. The central thesis of this science of character was that 'all productive labour that rises above the lowest is always motived by the desire for social inequality'.[92] Underlying these apparently shifting attitudes towards science lay Mallock's main purpose, which was centrally relevant to our concerns here. This was to denounce the assumption that social science could be made to reinforce the fashionable ethical assumptions of the age, which supposed the inevitability of progress towards greater equality. Mallock was, in other words, the most significant polemical opponent of the project of synthesizing positive social science and idealist ethics.

The main theme of Mallock's political and economic writings was that progress depends upon an inventive and entrepreneurial élite. He defined social evolution as 'the unintended result of the intentions of great men'.[93] The labour theory of value, upon which the Fabians now constructed their analysis, neglected the role of entrepreneurship. 'The sole cause . . . of this increment [in *per capita* wealth] has not been Labour, but the gradual concentration of the moral and intellectual faculties of exceptional men on the problem of directing Labour.'[94] The continuing advance of civilization depended fundamentally upon the preservation of inequality.

Mallock's emphasis upon the inevitability of economic and political inequality did not entail the simple assumption by conservatives of the doctrines of the classical economists; for the classical economists had generally assumed universal rationality. By contrast, Mallock exemplifies the critique of rationality which was an important feature of Conservative political thought at the end of the nineteenth century: it was echoed in the thinking of successive Unionist prime ministers, Salisbury and Balfour. It was not, of course, confined to Conservatives. It was present in the Fabian Graham Wallas's classic *Human Nature in Politics*. Furthermore, the notion that some of the poor were incapable of responding to the dictates of economic rationality was an important innovation in *fin-de-siècle* social investigation: this was the significance of the concept of the residuum – a sort of underclass – which permeated the work of the Charity Organization Society in the 1890s, though not earlier. But on the whole the faith in rationality remained much more resilient in British than in continental European social thought. There were no British Nietzsches or Sorels.

Stephen, Salisbury, Mallock and others mobilized moral and cognitive relativism in support of conservative political theory. But the notion that the state embodies ethical values was subjected to a very different line of attack by the important school of pluralist thinkers who came to prominence at the end of our period. These writers – the medieval historian F. W. Maitland (1850–1906) and the historian and divine J. N. Figgis (1866–1919), followed in the next generation by the academic socialists Harold Laski (1893–1950) and G. D. H. Cole (1889–1959) – occupy an interestingly ambiguous position in relation to the doctrines discussed in this chapter. At one level they owed a good deal to idealist insights: the critique of individualism and the affirmation of the moral personality of groups were common ground between idealists and pluralists. This was why a thinker such as Sir Ernest Barker could move so effortlessly from one camp to the other. What no pluralist could accept, however, was the primacy of the state; all attacked the concept of state sovereignty, a 'venerable fiction' in Figgis's view, and Figgis at least had a marked tendency to regard the state as an alien imposition on top of 'natural' social groupings such as families, churches and trade unions. These groups were not created by the state; rather, they arose from 'the natural associative instincts of mankind'; and they must therefore be respected by the state 'as having a life original and guaranteed'.[95] Maitland – a Cambridge man to the core, and Sidgwick's pupil – had particularly strong affinities with the sceptical intellectual style we have identified, and was healthily dismissive of idealist pieties.

Pluralism, more than any other doctrine, had the potential to put its finger on idealism's weak spot: its tendency to think of the human good as unitary in character, and its conflation of what is good for man with what is morally right. The pluralists, almost by definition, had a greater sense of the plurality of values, and this made them more willing to accept that conflict and competition might be productive. They thus heralded a reaction against the ethical bias that pervaded Victorian social thought.

This ethical bias used to be considered a fatal source of weakness in British intellectual culture. Perry Anderson, Philip Abrams and others attributed to it the failure to develop a properly sociological tradition; and Noel Annan developed a similar interpretation from a different intellectual standpoint.[96] But this line of argument now looks less appealing than it once did. It has become apparent from a number of recent studies that ethical concerns were by no means alien to late-Victorian and Edwardian projects to construct a 'social science'; conversely, they also underpinned the work of continental European pioneers of sociology from Comte to Durkheim. Moreover, it is practically a commonplace in the 1990s that attempts to reconstruct the progressive tradition in British politics must break with the mechanistic approach to social reform – arguably rooted in Fabianism – that prevailed in the 1960s, and must make space for the importance of ethical values and the moralizing importance of communities.[97] Perhaps, after all, the Bosanquets speak more directly to our age than do the Webbs.

NOTES

Notes to the Introduction

1. B. Bosanquet, 'The reality of the General Will', in B. Bosanquet (ed.), *Aspects of the Social Problem by Various Writers* (1895), pp. 319–32.
2. Thomas Carlyle, 'Signs of the Times' [from *Edinburgh Review*, 1829] in his *Critical and Miscellaneous Essays*, vol. II, pp. 313–42.
3. Frederick Maurice (ed.), *Life of Frederick Denison Maurice, Chiefly Told in his Own Letters*, vol. II, pp. 276, quoted in *DNB*. Maurice, *The Epistles of St John*, p. 344, quoted by J. B. Schneewind, 'Sidgwick and the Cambridge Moralists', in Bart Schultz (ed.), *Essays on Henry Sidgwick* (1992), p. 101.
4. J. R. Seeley, 'Ethics and Religion', in *Ethics and Religion* (1900), p. 11; Benjamin Kidd, *Social Evolution* (1894), p. 1.
5. Francis Galton, *English Men of Science: Their Nature and Nurture* (1874), p. 260.
6. Ernest Barker, *Political Thought in England from Herbert Spencer to the Present Day* (1915), pp. 12 and 250.
7. A. V. Dicey, *Lectures on the Relation between Law and Public Opinion in England during the Nineteenth Century* (2nd edn, 1914), p. 444. Cf. William Thomas, *The Philosophic Radicals: Nine Studies in Theory and Practice, 1817–1841* (1979), p. 6.
8. A. V. Dicey, *Law and Opinion*, pp. 438–9.
9. See, for example, Sheldon Wolin, *Politics and Vision: Continuity and Innovation in Western Political Thought* (1960), chs 9 and 10; W. G. Runciman, *Social Science and Political Theory* (1963), ch. 2.
10. Stefan Collini, Donald Winch and John Burrow, *That Noble Science of Politics: A Study in Nineteenth-Century Intellectual History* (1983).
11. Cf. Arthur Penrhyn Stanley, *Life and Correspondence of Thomas Arnold, D.D.* (n.d.), p. 122.
12. W. E. Gladstone, *Studies Subsidiary to the Works of Bishop Butler* (1896), p. 6.
13. Quoted in Jane Garnett, 'Hastings Rashdall and the Renewal of Christian Social Ethics, *c.* 1890–1920', in Jane Garnett and Colin Matthew (eds), *Revival and Religion since 1700: Essays for John Walsh* (1993), p. 307.

1 Economic Men: Political Economy and Political Thought

1. T. R. Malthus, *An Essay on the Principle of Population*, ed. D. Winch (1992), p. 343.
2. Michael Bentley, '"Boundaries" in Theoretical Language about the British State', in S. J. D. Green and R. C. Whiting (eds), *The Boundaries of the State in Modern Britain* (1996), p. 37.
3. F. D. Maurice, *Kingdom of Christ* [1838], 3rd edn (1883), vol. I, p. 218.
4. Elie Halévy, *The Growth of Philosophic Radicalism* [1928], 1972 edn, p. 6.
5. Jeremy Bentham, *An Introduction to the Principles of Morals and Legislation*, ed. J. H. Burns and H. L. A. Hart (1970), p. 11.
6. John Dinwiddy, *Bentham* (1989), pp. 27–8.
7. J. B. Schneewind, *Sidgwick's Ethics and Victorian Moral Philosophy* (1977), p. 129.
8. William Thomas, *Philosophic Radicals*, pp. 3–4.
9. *Ibid.*, pp. 7, 126–7.
10. *Ibid.*, p. 104.
11. D. Stewart, quoted in Stefan Collini, Donald Winch and John Burrow, *That Noble Science of Politics: A Study in Nineteenth-Century Intellectual History* (1983), p. 36.
12. D. Stewart, *Lectures on Political Economy*, quoted by Maxine Berg, *The Machinery Question and the Making of Political Economy, 1815–1848* (1980), p. 35.
13. Quoted in Collini *et al.*, *That Noble Science*, p. 61.
14. Jack Lively and John Rees (eds), *Utilitarian Logic and Politics: James Mill's 'Essay on government', Macaulay's Critique and the Ensuing Debate* (1978), p. 282.
15. Thomas, *Philosophic Radicals*, p. 129.
16. Lively and Rees, *Utilitarian Logic*, p. 124.
17. *Ibid.*, p. 170.
18. Gertrude Himmelfarb, *The Idea of Poverty: England in the Early Industrial Age* (1984), p. 100.
19. Boyd Hilton, *The Age of Atonement: The Influence of Evangelicalism on Social and Economic Thought* (1988), p. 3.
20. T. R. Malthus, *An Essay on the Principle of Population*, ed. D. Winch (1992), pp. 50–1.
21. Donald Winch, *Malthus* (1987), pp. 16–17.
22. Malthus to Whewell, 23 February 1831; quoted by Samuel Hollander, 'On Malthus's Population Principle and Social Reform', *History of Political Economy*, vol. 18.2 (1986), p. 187.
23. Winch, *Malthus*, p. 6.
24. Hilton, *Age of Atonement*, pp. 245, 248.
25. *Ibid.*, p. 91.
26. Peter Mandler, 'Debate: the Making of the New Poor Law *Redivivus*', *Past & Present*, no. 127 (May 1990), p. 201.
27. Mandler, 'Debate', p. 198.
28. Hilton, *Age of Atonement*, p. 93.
29. Samuel Leon Levy, *Nassau W. Senior, 1790–1864* (1970), pp. 200–201.

30. Halévy, *Growth of Philosophic Radicalism*, p. 281.
31. James J. Sack, *From Jacobite to Conservative: Reaction and Orthodoxy in Britain, c. 1760–1832* (1993), pp. 181, 183.
32. Anna Gambles, 'Rethinking the Politics of Protection: Conservatism and the Corn Laws, 1830–52', *English Historical Review*, vol. CXIII (1998), pp. 928–52.
33. A. Quinton, *The Politics of Imperfection* (1976), pp. 171–2.
34. *Coleridge's Writings*, vol. 1: *On Politics and Society*, ed. J. Morrow (1991), pp. 117–18 and 186–7.
35. Charles Richard Sanders, *Coleridge and the Broad Church Movement* (Durham, N.C., 1942), p. 53.
36. *Collected Works of John Stuart Mill* (1963–89), vol. X, p. 155.
37. *Coleridge's Writings*, vol. I, p. 187.
38. Thomas Carlyle, 'Signs of the Times' [1829], in *Critical and Miscellaneous Essays*, vol. II (1870), pp. 100–7.
39. Thomas Carlyle, *Past & Present* (1896 edn), p. 25.
40. Thomas Carlyle, *Sartor Resartus: The Life and Opinions of Herr Teufelsdröckh* (1896 edn), pp. 160–4.
41. 'Chartism', in A. Shelston (ed.), *Thomas Carlyle: Selected Writings* (1971), p. 189.
42. Carlyle, *Past & Present*, pp. 29, 126.
43. *Ibid.*, pp. 29, 117.
44. Carlyle, 'Chartism', p. 189.
45. *Ibid.*, 181–7.
46. *Ibid.*, p. 190.
47. Mill, *System of Logic* [*Collected Works* (*CW*), vol. VIII], pp. 879–80.
48. Mill, *Autobiography* [*CW* I], p. 166.
49. Mill, *System of Logic*, p. 879.
50. Mill, 'Bentham' [*CW* X], p. 99.
51. Quoted in Stefan Collini, *Liberalism and Sociology: L. T. Hobhouse and Political Argument in England* (1979), p. 29.
52. José Harris, *Private Lives, Public Spirit: A Social History of Britain, 1870–1914* (1993), p. 248.
53. Asa Briggs, *Victorian People: A Reassessment of People and Themes, 1851–67* (1965), p. 124.
54. *Ibid.*, pp. 125–6.
55. *Ibid.*, p. 133.
56. Samuel Smiles, *Self-Help: with Illustrations of Character and Conduct* (1859), p. 2.
57. Samuel Smiles, *Character* (1871), pp. 10–11.
58. Smiles, *Self-Help*, pp. 295, 301.
59. *Ibid.*, p. 295.
60. *Ibid.*, p. 3.
61. For these points see H. S. Jones, 'John Stuart Mill as Moralist', *Journal of the History of Ideas*, vol. 53 (1992), esp. p. 299.
62. Mill, 'Utility of Religion', *CW* X, p. 422.
63. Mill, *Autobiography*, pp. 239–41.
64. *Ibid.*, p. 177.
65. Mill, *On Liberty*, *CW* XVIII, p. 305.

66. Mill, 'Considerations on Representative Government', *CW* XIX, pp. 389–90.
67. *Ibid.*, p. 396.
68. Mill, *Principles of Political Economy*, *CW* III, p. 943.
69. *Ibid.*, p. 944.
70. I am indebted here to Barry Hindess, 'Liberalism, Socialism and Democracy: Variations on a Governmental Theme', in Andrew Barry, Thomas Osborne and Nikolas Rose (eds), *Foucault and Political Reason: Liberalism, Neo-liberalism and Rationalities of Government* (1996), pp. 65–80.

2   The State of the Nation: History, Culture and Democracy

1. Thomas Arnold, 'Appendix' to his inaugural lecture in *Introductory Lectures on Modern History*, 3rd edn (1845), p. 49.
2. 'The moral theory of a state, which I believe to be the foundation of political truth . . .' (Arnold, *Introductory Lectures*, p. 49).
3. *Ibid.*, pp. 38, 35.
4. *Ibid.*, pp. 39–40.
5. *Ibid.*, pp. 46–7.
6. 'Preface to the Third Volume of the Edition of Thucydides' [1835] in Arnold, *Miscellaneous Works* (1845), pp. 395–6.
7. Arnold to J. C. Hare, 12 May 1834: Arthur Penrhyn Stanley, *Life and Correspondence of Thomas Arnold D.D.* (n.d.), pp. 220–1.
8. Arnold to Whately, 4 May 1836: Stanley, *Life of Arnold*, p. 274.
9. Arnold, *Miscellaneous Works*, p. 110; C. R. Sanders, *Coleridge and the Broad Church Movement* (1942), p. 110.
10. Arnold to Bunsen, 6 May 1833: Stanley, *Life of Arnold*, p. 203.
11. Arnold to Bunsen, 10 February 1835: *ibid.*, pp. 235–6.
12. 'Postscript' to 'Principles of Church Reform', in Arnold, *Miscellaneous Works*, p. 331.
13. Maurice to Erskine, 8 August 1841: Sir John F. Maurice, *The Life of Frederick Denison Maurice* (1885) vol. I, p. 306.
14. F. D. Maurice, *The Kingdom of Christ* (3rd edn, 1883), vol. I, p. 222.
15. *Ibid.*, pp. 221–2.
16. Quoted by Alex R. Vidler, *F. D. Maurice and Company: Nineteenth Century Studies* (1966), pp. 161–2.
17. *Ibid.*, p. 163.
18. Arnold, *Miscellaneous Works*, p. 483.
19. Edward Norman, *The Victorian Christian Socialists* (1987), p. 38.
20. Maurice to Ludlow, 24 March 1848: Maurice, *Life of Maurice*, vol. i, p. 459.
21. Norman, *Christian Socialists*, p. 17.
22. Maurice, *The Kingdom of Christ*, vol. II, p. 337.
23. Norman, *Christian Socialists*, p. 40.
24. J. P. Parry, *Democracy and Religion: Gladstone and the Liberal Party, 1867–1875* (1986), pp. 72–3.
25. Quoted by J. W. Burrow, *A Liberal Descent: Victorian Historians and the English Past* (1981), p. 30.

26.   T. B. Macaulay, *History of England* (1906 edn), vol. I, p. 12.

27.   *Ibid.*, p. 13.

28.   Henry Hallam, *View of the State of Europe during the Middle Ages* [1818], 3rd edn 1853, vol. III, p. 158.

29.   Burrow, *Liberal Descent*, p. 47.

30.   P. B. M. Blaas, *Continuity and Anachronism: Parliamentary and Constitutional Development in Whig Historiography and in the Anti-Whig Reaction between 1890 and 1930* (1978), p. 117.

31.   Stefan Collini, Donald Winch and John Burrow, *That Noble Science*, p. 191.

32.   Blaas, *Continuity and Anachronism*, pp. 115–21.

33.   Quoted by Blaas, *op. cit.*, p. 117.

34.   A. O. Rutson, 'Opportunities and Shortcomings of Government in England' and J. Bryce, 'The Historical Aspect of Democracy', in *Essays on Reform* (1867), pp. 277, 283.

35.   Deborah Wormell, *Sir John Seeley and the Uses of History* (1980), p. 154.

36.   H. A. L. Fisher, 'Sir John Seeley', *Fortnightly Review*, vol. 60 (1896), p. 191; quoted by Wormell, *Seeley*, p. 155.

37.   John Robert Seeley, *Introduction to Political Science* (1896), p. 40.

38.   *Ibid.*, pp. 212–14.

39.   *Ibid.*, p. 236

40.   John Robert Seeley, *The Expansion of England* [1883], 2nd edn (1895), p. 10.

41.   R. Shannon, 'John Robert Seeley and the Idea of a National Church', in R. Robson (ed.), *Ideas and Institutions of Victorian Britain* (1967), p. 257; Seeley, *Expansion of England*, p. 9.

42.   John Robert Seeley, 'The Church as a Teacher of Morality', in W. L. Clay (ed.), *Essays on Church Policy* (1868), p. 291.

43.   Seeley, *Introduction to Political Science*, p. 35.

44.   Seeley, *The Expansion of England*, p. 13.

45.   Peter Cain, 'The Economic Philosophy of Constructive Imperialism', in Cornelia Navari (ed.), *British Politics and the Spirit of the Age: Political Concepts in Action* (1996), pp. 41–65.

46.   H. C. G. Matthew, 'Gladstone, Vaticanism, and the Question of the East', *Studies in Church History*, vol. XV (1978), pp. 418–19.

47.   W. E. Gladstone, *A Chapter of Autobiography* (1868), pp. 18–19.

48.   T. B. Macaulay, 'Gladstone on Church and State', *Edinburgh Review*, April 1839, reprinted in Macaulay's *Critical and Historical Essays* (1860), vol. II, pp. 51–2.

49.   *Ibid.*, pp. 78–80.

50.   Quoted by Perry Butler, *Gladstone: Church, State, and Tractarianism* (1982), p. 92.

51.   See H. C. G. Matthew, *Gladstone* (1988); also his 'Gladstone, Vaticanism, and the Question of the East'.

52.   Matthew, *Gladstone*, p. 76.

53.   Gladstone, *Chapter of Autobiography*, p. 28.

54.   Gladstone, *Vaticanism* (1875), p. 113

55.   Mill, *Considerations on Representative Government* (*CW* XIX), p. 547.

56.   J. E. D. Acton, 'Nationality', *Home and Foreign Review*, vol. I (1862), reprinted in Julia Stapelton (ed.), *Liberalism, Democracy, and the State in Britain: Five Essays, 1862–1891* (1997), p. 87.

57. *Ibid.*, p. 87.
58. Quoted by Ben Knights, *The Idea of the Clerisy in the Nineteenth Century* (1978), p. 107.
59. *Ibid.*, p. 115.
60. Quoted in *ibid.*, p. 120.
61. Matthew Arnold, 'The Literary Influence of Academies', *Cornhill Magazine* August 1864, in *Lectures and Essays in Criticism*, vol. III of *The Complete Prose Works of Matthew Arnold* (1962), pp. 235, 257.
62. Mill, *Later Letters (CW* IV), pp. 1936–8.
63. Walter Bagehot, *Physics and Politics*, in the *Collected Works of Walter Bagehot*, ed. Norman St John Stevas (1974), vol. VII, pp. 51–2.
64. Knights, *Idea of the Clerisy*, p. 123.
65. See Walter Bagehot, 'The Metaphysical Basis of Toleration', *Contemporary Review*, April 1874, in his *Literary Studies*, pp. 204–25.
66. Bagehot, *Physics and Politics*, p. 109.
67. Walter Bagehot, 'Why an English Liberal May Look without Disapproval on the Progress of Imperialism in France' [1874], in Norman St John-Stevas (ed.), *Bagehot's Historical Essays* (1971), p. 448.
68. Walter Bagehot, *The English Constitution*, in the *Collected Works of Walter Bagehot*, ed. Norman St John Stevas (1974) vol. V, p. 216.
69. *Ibid.*, p. 221.
70. J. Morley, *Life of Gladstone* (1922), vol. II, p. 520.
71. Walter Bagehot, 'Letters on the French coup d'état of 1851' [1852], in *Bagehot's Historical Essays* (1971), p. 401.
72. Keith Michael Baker, *Inventing the French Revolution: Essays on French Political Culture in the Eighteenth Century* (1990), p. 168.
73. J. P. Parry, *The Rise and Fall of Liberal Government in Victorian Britain* (1993), pp. 44–5.
74. Walter Bagehot, 'Intellectual conservatism', *Saturday Review*, 26 April 1856, in *Collected Works*, vol. VI, p. 98.
75. Walter Bagehot, review of Mill's *Considerations on Representative Government*, in *The Economist*, 11 May 1861, in *Collected Works*, vol. VI, p. 336.
76. Gladstone, *Chapter of Autobiography*, pp. 10–11.
77. *Ibid.*, pp. 11–12.
78. *Ibid.*, pp. 60–1.
79. Gertrude Himmelfarb, *Victorian Minds* (1968), p. 227.
80. Walter Bagehot, 'Parliamentary reform' [1859], in *Collected Works*, vol. VI, p. 193.
81. *Ibid.*, p. 235.
82. Martha Vogeler, *Frederic Harrison: the Vocations of a Positivist* (1984), p. 119.
83. Frederic Harrison, *Order and Progress*, p. 24, n. 1.
84. *Ibid.*, p. 349.
85. *Ibid.*, pp. 387–8.
86. *Ibid.*, p. 386.
87. Lord Houghton, 'On the Admission of the Working Classes as Part of our Social System, and on their Recognition for all Purposes as Part of the Nation', *Essays on Reform* (1867), p. 66.

3 The Discovery of Society: Evolution, Ethics and the State

1. Beatrice Webb, *My Apprenticeship* (1971), pp. 130 and 142–3.
2. Robert M. Young, 'Malthus and the Evolutionists: the Common Context of Biological and Social Theory', *Past & Present*, no. 43 (1969), pp. 109–45.
3. D. G. Ritchie, *Darwin and Hegel* (1893), p. 41.
4. D. G. Ritchie, 'The Moral Function of the State', in Michael Taylor (ed.), *Herbert Spencer and the Limits of the State: The Late Nineteenth-Century Debate between Individualism and Collectivism* (1996), p. 171.
5. Herbert Spencer, *Autobiography* (1904), vol. II, p. 103.
6. M. W. Taylor, *Men versus the State: Herbert Spencer and Late Victorian Individualism* (1992); and T. S. Gray, 'Herbert Spencer: Individualist or Organicist?', *Political Studies*, vol. 33 (1985), pp. 236–53.
7. Herbert Spencer, 'The Social Organism', in his *Essays: Scientific, Political and Speculative*, 2nd series (1868) vol. I, p. 396.
8. Herbert Spencer, *The Principles of Sociology* (1876), vol. I, p. 613.
9. Herbert Spencer, 'Progress: its Law and Cause', in his *Essays: Scientific, Political and Speculative*, 1st series (1858), p. 30.
10. Sidney Webb, 'Historic', in G. B. Shaw (ed.), *Fabian Essays* (1889), pp. 62–93.
11. J. R. Seeley, 'Ethics and Religion' [address to the Cambridge Ethical Society, 1888] in *Ethics and Religion* (1900), p. 6.
12. Marcus G. Singer, 'Sidgwick and Nineteenth-century British Ethical Thought', in Bart Schultz (ed.), *Essays on Henry Sidgwick* (1992), pp. 87–88.
13. J. Morley, *On Compromise* (1886), p. 29; quoted by Jeffrey Paul von Arx, *Progress and Pessimism: Religion, Politics, and History in Late-Nineteenth Century Britain* (1985), pp. 129, 154.
14. Leslie Stephen, *Social Rights and Duties* (1896), vol. I, pp. 35–6. Cf. also Noel Annan, *Leslie Stephen: The Godless Victorian* (1984), pp. 229–30.
15. Von Arx, *Progress and Pessimism*, p. 47.
16. *Ibid.*, pp. 51–4.
17. T. H. Huxley, *Evolution and Ethics and Oher Essays* (1906), p. 81.
18. Quoted by Annan, *Leslie Stephen*, p. 287.
19. T. H. Huxley, *Evolution and Ethics*, p. 58.
20. *Ibid.*, p. 83.
21. Benjamin Kidd, *Social Evolution* (1894), p. 5.
22. *Ibid.*, p. 1.
23. Quoted by D. P. Crook, *Benjamin Kidd: Portrait of a Social Darwinist* (1984), p. 53.
24. *Ibid.*, p. 54.
25. *Ibid.*, p. 157; cf. also Benjamin Kidd, *Principles of Western Civilisation* (1902), chs 10 and 11.
26. Kidd, *Social Evolution*, p. 237.
27. *Ibid.*, pp. 69 ff.
28. *Ibid.*, p. 78.
29. *Ibid.*, pp. 100–1.
30. Francis Galton, 'Eugenics: its Definition, Scope and Aims', *American Journal of Sociology*, vol. 10, no. 1 (July 1904), pp. 1–25.

31. See Sandra den Otter, *British Idealism and Social Explanation: A Study in Late Victorian Theory* (1996); José Harris, 'Political Thought and the Welfare State 1870–1940: an Intellectual Framework for British Social Policy', *Past & Present*, no. 135 (May 1992), pp. 116–141; *idem.*, 'The Webbs, the COS and the Ratan Tata Foundation', in Martin Bulmer, Jane Lewis and David Piachaud (eds), *The Goals of Social Policy* (1989), pp. 27–63.

32. Carl Schmitt, quoted by David Nicholls, *Deity and Domination: Images of God and the State in the Nineteenth and Twentieth Centuries* (1989), p. 13.

33. T. H. Green, *Lectures on the Principles of Political Obligation and Other Writings*, ed. P. Harris and J. Morrow (1986), p. 97.

34. *Ibid.*, p. 134.

35. T. H. Green, 'Lecture on "Liberal Legislation and Freedom of Contract"' [1881], *ibid.*, p. 199.

36. A. Toynbee, 'Notes and Jottings', in his *Lectures on the Industrial Revolution of the 18th Century in England: Popular Addresses, Notes and Other Fragments* (1884), p. 249.

37. A. Toynbee, 'The Ideal Relation of Church and State', in *ibid.*, pp. 238–9.

38. P. Hinchliff, *Benjamin Jowett and the Christian Religion* (1987), pp. 219–20.

39. T. H. Green, 'Lecture on "Liberal Legislation and Freedom of Contract"', in *Lectures on the Principles of Political Obligation and Other Writings*, p. 202.

40. Bernard Bosanquet, *The Philosophical Theory of the State* [1899] (4th edn, 1923), pp. 169, 178.

41. *Ibid.*, pp. 176, 180.

42. J. A. Hobson, *The Crisis of Liberalism: New Issues of Democracy* (1909), p. 187.

43. Bosanquet, *Philosophical Theory of the State*, p. 59

44. Carole Pateman, 'Feminist Critiques of the Public/Private Dichotomy', in Anne Phillips (ed.), *Feminism and Equality* (1987), p. 104.

45. Kate Millett, *Sexual Politics* (1977 edn), pp. 88–108.

46. Harriet Taylor Mill, 'Enfranchisement of Women', Appendix C in *Collected Works of John Stuart Mill*, vol. XXI, pp. 403–4.

47. J. S. Mill, 'The Subjection of Women', in *ibid.*, p. 297.

48. Richard W. Krouse, 'Patriarchal Liberalism and Beyond: from John Stuart Mill to Harriet Taylor', in Jean B. Elshtain (ed.), *The Family in Political Thought* (1982), p. 146.

49. Mill to Alexander Bain, 14 July 1869: *CW* XVIII, pp. 1623–4.

50. Barbara Caine, *Victorian Feminists* (1992), pp. 37–8.

51. Adam Kuper, 'The Rise and Fall of Maine's Patriarchal Society', in Alan Diamond (ed.), *The Victorian Achievement of Sir Henry Maine: a Centennial Reappraisal* (1991), p. 109.

52. F. D. Maurice, *Social Morality* (1893 edn), p. x.

53. Elizabeth Fee, 'The Sexual Politics of Victorian Social Anthropology', in Mary S. Hartman and Lois Banner (eds), *Clio's Consciousness Raised: New Perspectives on the History of Women* (1974), p. 88.

54. Sir Henry Sumner Maine, *Ancient Law* [1861] (1906 edn), p. 140.

55. Sir Henry Sumner Maine, *Lectures on the Early History of Institutions* (1875), p. 310.

56. *Ibid.*, pp. 326–7, 339.

57. Helen Bosanquet, *The Family* (1906), pp. v, 7.

58. *Ibid.*, p. 291.
59. *Ibid.*, pp. 244–5.
60. *Ibid.*, p. 298.
61. Olive Anderson, 'The Feminism of T. H. Green: a Late-Victorian Success Story', *History of Political Thought*, vol. XII (1991), p. 677.
62. Herbert Spencer, *Principles of Ethics* [1892–3] (1978 edn) vol. II, p. 216.
63. D. G. Ritchie, *Darwinism and Politics*, 2nd edn (1891), pp. 71–3.
64. Patrick Geddes and J. Arthur Thomson, *The Evolution of Sex* (1889), pp. 270–1.
65. José Harris, *Private Lives, Public Spirit: A Social History of Britain, 1870–1914* (1993), p. 229.
66. Millicent Garrett Fawcett, 'Home and Politics' [*c.* 1889–90] in Jane Lewis (ed.), *Before the Vote was Won: Arguments For and Against Women's Suffrage* (1987), pp. 418–24; Frances Power Cobbe, 'The Ethics of Zoophily', *Contemporary Review*, vol. LXVIII (1895), p. 497.
67. John Robert Seeley, *Ecce Homo* (Everyman edn), p. 130.
68. J. M. Keynes, 'Alfred Marshall, 1842–1924', in A. C. Pigou (ed.), *Memorials of Alfred Marshall* (1925), p. 56.
69. *Ibid.*, p. 10.
70. A. C. Pigou, 'In Memoriam: Alfred Marshall', in Pigou (ed.), *Memorials*, p. 82.
71. Alfred Marshall, *Principles of Economics* (1890), vol. I, p. 1.
72. Alfred Marshall, 'The Present Condition of Economics' [1885], in Pigou (ed.), *Memorials*.
73. Alfred Marshall, *Official Papers* (1926), p. 201.
74. Marshall to Helen Bosanquet, 28 September 1902; reprinted in Pigou (ed.), *Memorials*, pp. 443–4.
75. For this argument see Daniel Pick, *Faces of Degeneration* (1989).
76. On this episode see R. Skidelsky, *John Maynard Keynes*, vol. 1: *Hopes Betrayed, 1883–1920* (1983), pp. 223–6.
77. Marshall, *Principles of Economics*, p. 78.
78. *Ibid.*, pp. 82–3.
79. *Ibid.*, pp. 592–3.
80. *Ibid.*, pp. 123, 252–3.
81. F. Y. Edgeworth, 'Reminiscences', in Pigou (ed.), *Memorials*, pp. 72–3. On Marshall's ideas about the family, see especially Peter Groenewegen, 'Alfred Marshall – Women and Economic Development: Labour, Family and Race', in Groenewegen (ed.), *Feminism and Political Economy in Victorian England* (1994); also Michèle Pujol, 'Gender and Class in Marshall's *Principles of Economics*', *Cambridge Journal of Economics*, vol. VIII (1984), pp. 217–34.
82. Herbert Spencer, *The Man versus the State* (1884), p. 6.
83. Sir J. F. Stephen, *Liberty, Equality, Fraternity* (1873), ed. R. J. White, p. 52.
84. Quoted in K. J. M. Smith, *James Fitzjames Stephen: Portrait of a Victorian Rationalist* (1988), p. 202.
85. Stephen, *Liberty, Equality, Fraternity*, p. 202.
86. *Saturday Review*, vol. 19 (1865); quoted by Michael Pinto-Duschinsky, *The Political Thought of Lord Salisbury, 1854–68* (1967), p. 76.
87. *Quarterly Review*, October 1867, reprinted in Paul Smith (ed.), *Lord Salisbury on Politics* (1972), p. 258.

88. Pinto-Duschinsky, *Political Thought of Lord Salisbury*, p. 112.
89. Henry Sidgwick, *The Elements of Politics* (1891), p. 2.
90. *Ibid.*, p. 45.
91. W. H. Mallock, *Studies in Contemporary Superstition* (1895), p. 205.
92. W. H. Mallock, *Social Equality: A Short Study in a Missing Science* (1882), pp. 100, 135–6.
93. W. H. Mallock, *Aristocracy and Evolution: A Study of the Rights, the Origin, and the Social Functions of the Wealthier Classes* (1898), p. 105.
94. Mallock, *Studies in Contemporary Superstition*, p. 249.
95. J. N. Figgis, *Churches in the Modern State* (1913), p. 47, quoted by Rodney Barker, *Political Ideas in Modern Britain* (1978), p. 96.
96. Perry Anderson, 'Components of the National Culture', *New Left Review*, no. 50 (July–August 1968), pp. 3–57; Philip Abrams, *The Origins of British Sociology, 1834–1914* (1968); Noel Annan, *The Curious Strength of Positivism in English Political Thought* (1959).
97. David Marquand, 'Moralists and Hedonists', in David Marquand and Anthony Seldon (eds), *The Ideas that Shaped Post-war Britain* (1996), pp. 5–28.

CHRONOLOGY

1776   Smith's *Inquiry into the Nature and Causes of the Wealth of Nations*; Bentham's *Fragment on Government*.
1789   Outbreak of French Revolution. Bentham's *Introduction to the Principles of Morals and Legislation*.
1790   Burke's *Reflections on the Revolution in France*.
1798   Malthus's first *Essay on the Principle of Population*.
1828   Repeal of Test and Corporation Acts: nonconformists admitted to parliament.
1829   Catholic Emancipation opens most public offices to Catholics.
1830   Coleridge's *Constitution of Church and State*.
1832   First Reform Act enfranchises large towns, standardizes franchise in boroughs, and increases size of electorate.
1833   Carlyle's *Sartor Resartus*.
1834   Poor Law Amendment Act.
1837   Accession of Queen Victoria.
1838   National Charter drawn up to formulate Chartist demands. Anti-Corn Law League set up. Gladstone's *The State in its Relations with the Church*. Maurice's *Kingdom of Christ*.
1839   Carlyle's *Chartism*.
1842   Thomas Arnold's *Introductory Lectures on Modern History*.
1843   Mill's *System of Logic*. Carlyle's *Past and Present*.
1846   Repeal of the Corn Laws; Conservatives split.
1848   Revolutions in continental Europe; collapse of Chartism in England. Mill's *Principles of Political Economy*. First volumes of Macaulay's *History of England*.
1859   Mill's *On Liberty*. Darwin's *Origin of Species*. Smiles's *Self-Help*.
1861   Maine's *Ancient Law*.
1867   Second Reform Act introduces householder franchise in boroughs. Bagehot's *English Constitution*.
1869   Disestablishment of the Irish Church. Mill's *Subjection of Women*. Arnold's *Culture and Anarchy*.
1872   Bagehot's *Physics and Politics*.
1873   Stephen's *Liberty, Equality, Fraternity*.
1874   Sidgwick's *Methods of Ethics*.
1881   Irish Land Act effectively allows landlord–tenant relations to be determined by agrarian custom rather than freedom of contract.
1883   Seeley's *Expansion of England*.

1884   Third Reform Act creates uniform franchise in boroughs and counties.
       Fabian Society founded. Spencer's *The Man versus the State*.
1885   Redistribution Act adopts principle of equal-sized constituencies.
1886   Gladstone's first Irish Home Rule Bill defeated; Liberals split. Green's
       posthumous *Lectures on the Principles of Political Obligation*.
1887   Formation of the Independent Labour Party.
1889   *Fabian Essays*. London dock strike.
1890   Marshall's *Principles of Economics*.
1893   Huxley's Romanes lecture, 'Evolution and Ethics'.
1894   Harcourt's budget introduces death duties. Kidd's *Social Evolution*.
1899   Bosanquet's *Philosophical Theory of the State*.
1901   Death of Queen Victoria.

GUIDE TO LEADING THINKERS

ACTON, Sir John Emerich Dalberg (1st Baron Acton) (1834–1902), historian, journalist, and liberal Catholic publicist. Whig MP (1859–65), Regius Professor of History at Cambridge (1895–1902). A prolific essayist who never completed a projected history of freedom. A liberal in the Whig tradition, his critique of unlimited popular sovereignty and his conviction that liberty depended on countervailing powers made him a forerunner of political pluralism.

ARNOLD, Matthew (1822–88), poet and critic, son of THOMAS ARNOLD. Author notably of *Culture and Anarchy* (1869). A cultural critic of democracy and radicalism from a national-liberal standpoint.

ARNOLD, Revd Dr Thomas (1795–1842), Liberal Anglican clergyman, historian, and reforming Headmaster of Rugby School (1828–42). Author of *Principles of Church Reform* (1833), *History of Rome* (1838–40), and *Introductory Lectures on Modern History* (1842). His historical works introduced German scholarship (e.g., Niebuhr) and the philosophy of Vico into England. He was the father of MATTHEW ARNOLD.

BAGEHOT, Walter (1826–77), political and economic journalist and critic. Author of *The English Constitution* (1867), in which he distinguished between the myth and the reality of British government, and *Physics and Politics* (1872), which explored the implications of **Darwinian** ideas for social and political thought. Editor of *The Economist* (1860–77).

BENTHAM, Jeremy (1748–1832), legal philosopher, commonly regarded as the founder of **utilitarianism**. Author of *A Fragment on Government* (1776) and *Introduction to the Principles of Morals and Legislation* (1789).

BOSANQUET, Bernard (1848–1923), idealist philosopher, a pupil of GREEN. A Liberal, in some ways an advanced one, but an opponent of collectivism, he was active in the Charity Organization Society and in the London Ethical Society. Author of *The Philosophical Theory of the State* (1899). His wife, HELEN BOSANQUET, née Dendy (1860–1925), was also active in the COS and wrote extensively on social and moral questions, e.g., *The Strength of the People* (1902) and *The Family* (1906).

BURKE, Edmund (1729–97), Whig politician. His *Reflections on the Revolution in France* (1790) defended the idea of a mixed constitution grounded in history against the novel claims of political radicalism. He is generally acknowledged to be one of the great theorists of British conservatism, although for most of the nineteenth century he was more popular with Whigs and Liberals than with Tories.

CARLYLE, Thomas (1795–1881), historian and critic, influential exponent of German literature and thought. Works included *Sartor Resartus* (1833), *The French Revolution* (1837), *Chartism* (1839) and *Past and Present* (1843).

COLERIDGE, Samuel Taylor (1772–1834), **romantic** poet and philosophical disciple of **Kant**; important in introducing German thought into England. Political writings included *Lay Sermons* (1816–17) and *The Constitution of Church and State* (1830). A critic of **utilitarianism** and political economy, his theological writings also influenced **Liberal Anglicanism**.

COMTE, Auguste (1798–1857), French philosopher and pioneer of sociology, best known as the founder of **positivism**. Served (1817–24) as secretary to Saint-Simon, who shaped the direction of his thinking. His major works, *Course of Positive Philosophy* (1830–42) and *System of Positive Polity* (1851–4), had a powerful influence on Victorian intellectual life.

DARWIN, Charles (1809–82), naturalist, famous chiefly for his theory of the transmutation or 'evolution' of species, which he set out in his *Origin of Species by Means of Natural Selection* (1859). There were numerous attempts to apply his ideas to politics and society, mostly in ways of which he disapproved. See **Darwinism**.

DICEY, Albert Venn (1835–1922), jurist, Vinerian Professor of English Law at Oxford from 1882 to 1909. His *Introduction to the Study of the Law of the Constitution* (1885) provided a classical exposition of the concept of parliamentary sovereignty. In his *Lectures on the Relation between Law and Public Opinion in England during the Nineteenth Century* (1905) he lamented the demise of Benthamite and classical economic certainties in public policy. An advanced liberal in the 1860s, he later became a trenchant advocate of the Unionist cause: in *England's Case against Home Rule* (1886) he argued that Home Rule for Ireland would endanger parliamentary sovereignty.

FIGGIS, Revd John Neville (1866–1919), historian and theologian, member of the Anglo-Catholic Community of the Resurrection at Mirfield. A leading advocate of political **pluralism** and critic of the concept of sovereignty, for example in his *Churches in the Modern State* (1913).

GLADSTONE, William Ewart (1809–98), statesman. Entered parliament as a Conservative, subsequently a Peelite, then Liberal Prime Minister (1868–74, 1880–5, 1886, 1892–4). A High Churchman, author of *The State in its Relations with the Church*, which argued for the organic bond between state and national church; later a critic of the ecclesiastical establishment on High Church grounds. Wrote extensively on theological and classical subjects.

GREEN, Thomas Hill (1836–82), philosopher, fellow of Balliol College and founder of Oxford **idealism**. Active on the radical wing of Liberalism.

Exerted a powerful personal sway over his pupils, but his main works were published after his early death: these included *Lectures on the Principles of Political Obligation* (1886). A critic of the **individualism** of the **utilitarian** school, he was a major intellectual influence on late-Victorian and Edwardian Liberalism.

HARRISON, Frederic (1831–1923), leading English advocate of **positivism**. Politically he began as an advanced Liberal, but the conservative implications of his thought became evident in works such as *Order and Progress* (1875).

HEGEL, Georg Wilhelm Friedrich (1770–1831), German philosopher, and the most important exponent of **idealist** political thought. In his *Philosophy of Right* (1821) and other works, he depicted the state as an ethical entity, and argued that true freedom could only be attained in and through the state. He had a significant but sometimes exaggerated influence on the idealists of late-Victorian Britain.

HUXLEY, Thomas Henry (1825–95), scientist. Best known as a polemicist in the **Darwinian** cause, but Romanes lecture at Oxford on 'Evolution and ethics' (1893) articulated his scepticism about the capacity of evolutionary biology to solve ethical questions.

KANT, Immanuel (1724–1804), German philosopher, by common consent the greatest philosopher of modern times. Although he was a political theorist of some significance, his importance for the student of Victorian Britain lies in his general philosophy. In his *Critique of Pure Reason* (1781) he rebutted empiricist claims and argued that knowledge of the world is possible because the self determines the structure of our experience. As a moral philosopher, in the *Critique of Practical Reason* (1788) and the *Groundwork of the Metaphysic of Morals*, he set out to defend the rationality of morality, which is not reducible to sentiment or fashion.

KIDD, Benjamin (1858–1916), minor civil servant who achieved celebrity and fortune with his *Social Evolution* (1894), in which he argued that the progress of the race depended on conditions which were irrational when considered from the point of view of the interests of the individuals of the present generation. Religion alone could persuade the individuals of the present to submit to the necessary sacrifices.

MACAULAY, Thomas Babington (1800–59), historian and politician. Prolific contributor to the Whig *Edinburgh Review* and author of a best-selling *History of England* (1848–55). MP with interruptions from 1830 to 1856, created Baron Macaulay 1857. Leading exponent of Whig interpretation of English history.

MAINE, Sir Henry Sumner (1822–88), jurist, held chairs at both Oxford and Cambridge, Master of Trinity Hall, Cambridge (1877–88). Famous for the application of the historical method to legal and political institutions, most importantly in his influential *Ancient Law* (1861), where he depicted social progress as a movement from relations based on status to relations based on contract. His work had a profound impact on fields other than the law, such as history, social theory and early anthropology. His Conservative political views were articulated chiefly in *Popular Government* (1885), where he depicted untrammelled democracy as a threat to progress.

MALTHUS, Revd Thomas Robert (1766–1834), Anglican clergyman and economist. Author notably of *An Essay on the Principle of Population* (1798), which argued that population growth naturally tended to outrun subsistence and therefore restricted the possibility of permanently raising the living standards of the poor. A second version of the essay (1803) was more optimistic in tone. His teaching had a profound impact on nineteenth-century systems of poor relief, e.g. the new poor law of 1834.

MARSHALL, Alfred (1842–1924), economist, professor of political economy at Cambridge (1884–1908). His *Principles of Economics* (1890) was the first great synthesis of the subject since MILL.

MAURICE, Revd Frederick Denison (1805–72), Anglican theologian and social critic. A follower of COLERIDGE, founder of Christian Socialism, and proponent of liberal theological teachings. Author of *The Kingdom of Christ* (1838), *Moral and Metaphysical Philosophy* (1854), and many other works.

MILL, James (1773–1836), historian, journalist, and **utilitarian** philosopher; friend and disciple of BENTHAM. Works included *History of India* (1818) and an 'Essay on Government' in the *Encyclopaedia Britannica* (1820). The father of JOHN STUART MILL, whom he educated personally.

Mill, John Stuart (1806–73), philosopher and economist, son of the **utilitarian** JAMES MILL. Author of numerous works, including *A System of Logic* (1843), *Principles of Political Economy* (1848), *On Liberty* (1859), *Considerations on Representative Government* (1861), The *Subjection of Women* (1869) and an *Autobiography* (1873). Liberal MP for Westminster (1865–8). He married Harriet Taylor (1807–58) in 1851. He set out to enhance the authoritative standing of the utilitarian system by broadening it to incorporate insights from **romanticism** and **historicism**.

SEELEY, Sir John Robert (1834–95), historian. A **Liberal Anglican**, he was the author of a controversial and best-selling life of Jesus, *Ecce Homo* (1865). Subsequently turned to modern political history in *The Life and Times of Stein* (1878), *The Expansion of England* (1883), and *Lectures on Political Science* (1896). He was a Liberal, and later a Liberal Unionist, in politics, and an advocate of imperial federation.

SIDGWICK, Henry (1838–1900), Cambridge philosopher who defended a subtle and modified form of **utilitarianism** against its **idealist** critics, notably in *Methods of Ethics* (1874). In politics he began as a Liberal but broke with the party over Irish Home Rule and became a Liberal Unionist.

SMILES, Samuel (1812–1904), journalist and popular writer, author of *Lives of the Engineers* (1861–2), *Self-Help* (1859) and *Character* (1871). Popularizer of **individualistic** values of industrial England.

SMITH, Adam (1723–90), economist and moral philosopher, author of *An Inquiry into the Nature and Causes of the Wealth of Nations* (1776). The father of classical economics and of the doctrine of *laissez-faire*. He held that, given a framework of law and government, individuals who pursue their own interest are led by an 'invisible hand' simultaneously to promote the common good.

SPENCER, Herbert (1820–1903), philosopher and sociologist who devoted his work to the creation of a grand intellectual synthesis based on the theory of evolution. In politics he was a Liberal whose extreme anti-**collectivism** came to seem increasingly conservative in its implications towards the end of his life. Works included *Principles of Sociology* (1876) and *The Man versus the State* (1884).

STEPHEN, Sir James Fitzjames (1829–94), lawyer, High Court judge and journalist. A prolific contributor to the *Saturday Review*, he was an old Liberal who considered himself faithful to BENTHAM, and in his *Liberty, Equality, Fraternity* (1873) denounced the optimism MILL's Liberalism. Brother of SIR LESLIE STEPHEN.

STEPHEN, Sir Leslie (1832–1904), historian and man of letters, founder and editor of the *Dictionary of National Biography*. A pioneer of the history of ideas in his *History of English Thought in the Eighteenth Century* (1876) and *The English Utilitarians* (1900), he also tried to apply evolutionary ideas to ethics in his *Science of Ethics* (1882). Brother of SIR JAMES FITZJAMES STEPHEN.

WEBB, Sidney (1859–1947), Socialist thinker and activist, co-founder of the **Fabian** Society, the London School of Economics, and the *New Statesman*; later a Labour MP and cabinet minister; created Baron Passfield in 1929. He was a contributor to *Fabian Essays* (1889). His wife BEATRICE WEBB (née Potter) (1858–1943) was his close intellectual collaborator, whose *My Apprenticeship* (1926) gives unique insight into the intellectual history of the later Victorian period.

GLOSSARY OF TERMS

This is not intended as a comprehensive glossary, but as an aid to understanding. It therefore provides short explanations of concepts with which some readers may be unfamiliar, and does not discuss familiar but contestable terms such as 'liberalism', 'conservatism' and 'democracy'.

Atomism   The belief that individuals are the only real entities in society, and that society has no legitimate ends distinct from those of the individuals composing it.

Collectivism   The belief in the pursuit of social goals through common action, and normally through the agency of the state. In late Victorian political argument it generally stood in contrast to **individualism**.

Darwinism   Theory of evolution derived from the work of Charles DARWIN, who argued that evolution proceeds by natural selection, so that those types of the species survive which are best adapted to the demands of their environment ('the survival of the fittest'). This contrasts with the theory developed by the Frenchman Lamarck, for whom the inheritance of acquired characteristics was the key mechanism of the evolution of species. Darwinian ideas were applied to society and politics in the form of the doctrine known as Social Darwinism. This taught that societies, like species, are subject to the law of evolution by natural selection. However, many so-called Social Darwinists in fact understood the mechanism of social evolution in Lamarckian terms.

Empiricism   The philosophical doctrine that experience constitutes the sole source of knowledge of the world. In Victorian Britain its leading exponents included J. S. MILL, whose *System of Logic* (1843) was an extended rebuttal of the doctrines of the rival school of intuitionists, who took the broadly **idealist** position that *a-priori* knowledge of the world is possible.

Fabianism   Form of socialism associated with the Fabian Society (founded 1884). It advocated the achievement of socialist ends by gradual reform through existing institutions. Its most influential early members included Sidney and Beatrice WEBB, H. G. Wells and G. B. Shaw.

Historicism   The doctrine, owing much to German **romanticism** and **idealism**, which taught that social and political phenomena could be understood only in relation to their place in history. It was commonly associated, as in COMTE, with the concept of a social system consisting of interdependent parts.

Idealism   The philosophical doctrine that mind is all that really exists. Its nine-teenth-century adherents owed most to KANT (1724–1804) and HEGEL (1770–1831), but perhaps most of all to Plato. Idealists rejected the **empiricist** teaching that all knowledge comes from experience, and instead stressed the active role of the mind in interpreting sense-experience. In Britain, idealist doctrines were propounded by COLERIDGE, CARLYLE and other Germanizers, and later by GREEN, BOSANQUET and BRADLEY. It became something of a philosophical orthodoxy in the late-Victorian period, especially at Oxford.

Individualism   This term is used in a range of distinct senses. One sense is 'methodological individualism': the doctrine that social explanation must ulti-mately be reducible to the explanation of individual behaviour. This is closely connected with **atomism**. A second sense refers to the romantic belief that the full flowering of the potential of individual human beings constitutes the supreme good: this was the core argument of J. S. MILL'S *On Liberty*. But in Victorian polit-ical argument the term usually referred to the classical liberal belief in a minimal role for the state, and was taken to be the opposite of **collectivism**. Individualists in this sense held that the general good was most likely to be promoted if individ-uals were, as far as possible, left to look after their own interests.

Liberal Anglicanism   Theological stance associated with the 'Broad Church' strand in the Church of England, and contrasted with Evangelicalism on the one hand and Anglo-Catholicism on the other. Liberal Anglicans (e.g. Thomas ARNOLD) upheld the established church but argued for doctrinal latitude. They argued that the essence of Christianity consisted of moral teachings rather than dogma.

Organicism   In social and political theory, the belief that the state or society possesses a systematic unity comparable to that of organisms in the natural world. This was a fashionable doctrine in the late Victorian and Edwardian period, but there was little agreement about its political implications.

Pluralism   In political thought, a doctrine which affirms the reality of group life and maintains that in a well-ordered society power is distributed among a wide range of groups. It challenges individualism on the one hand and the sovereign state on the other. Pluralist political theory flourished in early twentieth-century Britain, under the influence of such writers as FIGGIS and Cole.

Positivism   A doctrine, immensely influential in the nineteenth century, derived from the work of Auguste COMTE and his mentor Saint-Simon. Positivists held that in the modern age all true knowledge has to be scientific or 'positive': it must take the form of laws describing the coexistence or succession of observable phenomena. 'Theological' and 'metaphysical' forms of belief were outdated; but religion was a universal need, and positivists in Britain as elsewhere adhered to the 'religion of humanity' instituted by Comte.

Romanticism   A cultural movement, rather than a systematic doctrine, which had its origins in late eighteenth-century Germany in a rebellion against aspects of Enlightenment rationalism. Its main features included a rejection of abstract, classical and mechanical modes of thought, and a rehabilitation of nature, sim-plicity and feeling. British followers of romanticism included Wordsworth, COLERIDGE and CARLYLE.

Utilitarianism An ethical doctrine which takes the supreme good to be 'the greatest happiness of the greatest number'. In the hands of BENTHAM, James MILL and John Stuart MILL, it became an integral part of a radical liberal creed (sometimes known as Benthamism or philosophic radicalism), but it could also be deployed for more conservative purposes, as it was by William Paley and Henry SIDGWICK.

FURTHER READING

In the history of ideas, even for the callowest undergraduate there is no substitute for direct contact with primary texts. Fortunately there is a plentiful supply of good modern editions, and this reading list gives priority to texts that are readily available, and supplements them with a highly selective indication of the main secondary works. The Cambridge University Press's Cambridge Texts in the History of Political Thought (CTHPT), for example, includes texts by Mill, Arnold, Spencer, Hobhouse and a growing number of other Victorian thinkers. Mention should also be made of the excellent Key Issues series recently launched by Thoemmes Press: these volumes reprint contemporary responses to fundamental works by such thinkers as Mill and Spencer, and thus enable students to encounter a debate in accessible form. For reliable introductory accounts of leading thinkers, the student may be directed towards the Past Masters series published by the Oxford University Press.

General

The best point of entry to the study of Victorian intellectual history is by way of two incomparable intellectual autobiographies:

J. S. Mill, *Autobiography*, ed. J. Stillinger (1971).
Beatrice Webb, *My Apprenticeship* (Penguin, 1971).

Beyond that, there are surprisingly few general surveys of the subject; but the following should help:

Bellamy, Richard (ed.), *Victorian Liberalism: Nineteenth-Century Political Thought and Practice* (1990).
Bellamy, Richard, *Liberalism and Modern Society* (1992).
Bowle, John, *Politics and Opinion in the Nineteenth Century: An Historical Introduction* (1954).
Collini, Stefan, *Public Moralists: Political Thought and Intellectual Life in Britain, 1850–1930* (1991).
Collini, S., Winch D. and Burrow, J., *That Noble Science of Politics: A Study in Nineteenth-Century Intellectual History* (1983). A major work.
Francis, Mark and Morrow, John, *A History of British Political Thought in the Nineteenth Century* (1994). A valuable recent synthesis.

Gilmour, Robin, *The Victorian Period: The Intellectual and Cultural Context of English Literature, 1830–1890* (1993).
Himmelfarb, Gertrude, *Victorian Minds* (1968).
Mandelbaum, Maurice, *History, Man and Reason: A Study in Nineteenth-Century Thought* (1971).
Pearson, Robert and Williams, Geraint, *Political Thought and Public Policy in the Nineteenth Century: An Introduction* (1984).
de Ruggiero, Guido, *A History of European Liberalism*, trans. R. G. Collingwood (1927).
Turner, Frank M., *Contesting Cultural Authority: Essays in Victorian Intellectual Life* (1993).

1 Economic Men

Primary sources

Coleridge, S. T., *On the Constitution of Church and State* (ed. J. Barrell, 1972).
Jay, Elisabeth and Jay, Richard (eds), *Critics of Political Economy: Victorian Reactions to 'Political Economy'* (1986).
Lively, J., and Rees, J. C., *Utilitarian Logic and Politics: James Mill's 'Essay on Government', Macaulay's Critique, and the Ensuing Debate* (1978).
Mill, J. S., *Principles of Political Economy*, ed. D. Winch (1985). Winch's introduction gives splendid insight into Mill's thought.
Mill, J. S., *On Liberty and Other Writings* (CTHPT, ed. S. Collini, 1989).
Morrow, John (ed.), *Coleridge's Writings*, vol. 1: *On Politics and Society* (1990).
Pyle, Andrew (ed.), *On Liberty: Contemporary Responses to John Stuart Mill* (Key Issues, 1994).
Shelston, A. (ed.), *Thomas Carlyle: Selected Writings* (1971).
Smiles, Samuel, *Self-Help with Illustrations of Conduct and Perseverance* (IEA, 1996).

Secondary

Berg, Maxine, *The Machinery Question and the Making of Political Economy* (1980).
Burrow, John, *Whigs and Liberals: Continuity and Change in English Political Thought* (1988).
Dinwiddy, John, *Bentham* (1989).
Fontana, Biancamaria, *Rethinking the Politics of Commercial Society* (1985).
Halévy, Elie, *The Growth of Philosophic Radicalism* (1972).
Himmelfarb, Gertrude, *The Idea of Poverty: England in the Early Industrial Age* (1984).
Hilton, Boyd, *The Age of Atonement: The Influence of Evangelicalism on Social and Economic Thought, 1785–1865* (1988).
Robson, John M., *The Improvement of Mankind: The Social and Political Thought of John Stuart Mill* (1968).
Ryan, Alan, *The Philosophy of John Stuart Mill* (1970).
Skorupski, John (ed.), *The Cambridge Companion to Mill* (1998).
Waterman, A. M. C., *Revolution, Economics and Religion: Christian Political Economy, 1798–1833* (1991).

Thomas, William, *The Philosophic Radicals* (1979).
Thomas, William, *Mill* (1985).
Winch, Donald, *Malthus* (1987).
Winch, Donald, *Riches and Poverty: An Intellectual History of Political Economy in Britain, 1750–1834* (1996).

2   The State of the Nation

Primary

Arnold, Matthew, *Culture and Anarchy and Other Writings*, CTHPT, ed. S. Collini (1993).
Arnold, Thomas, *Introductory Lectures on Modern History*, 3rd edn (1845).
Bagehot, W., *The English Constitution*, ed. R. H. S. Crossman (1963).
Bagehot, W., *Physics and Politics*, in *The Collected Works of Walter Bagehot*, ed. Norman St John Stevas (1974), vol. 3.
Harrison, Frederic, *Order and Progress*, ed. Martha S. Vogeler (1975).
Macaulay, T. B., *The History of England from the Accession of James II* (1848 and numerous subsequent editions).
Maine, Sir Henry, *Ancient Law* (1861).
Maurice, F. D., *The Kingdom of Christ*, 2 vols (1838).
Seeley, J. R., *The Expansion of England* (1883).
Seeley, J. R., *Introduction to Political Science* (1896).
Stapleton, Julia (ed.), *Liberalism, Democracy, and the State in Britain: Five Essays, 1862–1891* (1997). This includes Acton on 'Nationality' and Dicey on 'The balance of classes'.

Secondary

Burrow, John, *A Liberal Descent: Victorian Historians and the English Past* (1981).
Culler, A. Dwight, *The Victorian Mirror of History* (1985).
Forbes, Duncan, *The Liberal Anglican Idea of History* (1952). A fundamental work.
Harvie, Christopher, *The Lights of Liberalism: University Liberals and the Challenge of Democracy, 1860–86* (1976).
Knights, Ben, *The Idea of the Clerisy in the Nineteenth Century* (1978).
Parry, J. P., *Democracy and Religion: Gladstone and the Liberal Party, 1867–1875* (1986). The best discussion of the relationship between religion and political thought, especially among the 'Whig-Liberals'.
Shannon, Richard, 'John Robert Seeley and the Idea of a National Church', in Robert Robson (ed.), *Ideas and Institutions of Victorian Britain* (1967), pp. 236–67.
Vogeler, Martha, *Frederic Harrison: The Vocations of a Positivist* (1984).
von Arx, Jeffrey Paul, *Progress and Pessimism: Religion, Politics, and History in Late-Nineteenth-Century Britain* (1985).

3 The Discovery of Society

Primary

Bagehot, W., *Physics and Politics* (1873).
Bosanquet, Bernard, *The Philosophical Theory of the State* (1899).
Boucher, David (ed.), *The British Idealists*, CTHPT (1997).
Green, T. H., *Lectures on the Principles of Political Obligation and Other Writings*, ed. P. Harris and J. Morrow (1986).
Huxley, T. H., *Evolution and Ethics* (1893).
Kidd, B., *Social Evolution* (1894).
Marshall, Alfred, *Principles of Economics* (1890).
Pyle, Andrew (ed.), *The Subjection of Women: Contemporary Responses to John Stuart Mill* (Key Issues, 1995).
Ritchie, D. G., *Darwinism and Politics* (1889).
Shaw, G. B. (ed.), *Fabian Essays* (1889).
Spencer, Herbert, *Political Writings*, CTHPT, ed. John Offer (1994).
Stapleton, Julia (ed.), *Liberalism, Democracy and the State in Britain: Five Essays, 1862–1891* (1997). This reprints, among other things, T. H. Green on 'Liberal Legislation and Freedom of Contract', and Herbert Spencer, 'From Freedom to Bondage'.
Stephen, Sir J. F., *Liberty, Equality, Fraternity* (Chicago, 1991).
Stephen, L., *The Science of Ethics* (1882).
Taylor Mill, Harriet and J. S. Mill, *The Enfranchisement of Women and the Subjection of Women*, ed. K. Soper (London, 1983).
Taylor, M. W. (ed.), *Herbert Spencer and the Limits of the State: The Late Nineteenth-Century Debate between Individualism and Collectivism* (1996).

Secondary

Annan, Noel, *Leslie Stephen: The Godless Victorian* (1984).
Burrow, J. W., *Evolution and Society: A Study in Victorian Social Theory* (1966).
Collini, Stefan, *Liberalism and Sociology: L. T. Hobhouse and Political Argument in England, 1880–1914* (1979).
Freeden, Michael, *The New Liberalism: An Ideology of Social Reform* (1978).
Meadowcroft, James, *Conceptualizing the State: Innovation and Dispute in British Political Thought, 1880–1914* (1995).
den Otter, Sandra, *British Idealism and Social Explanation: A Study in Late Victorian Thought* (1996).
Peel, J. D. Y., *Herbert Spencer: The Evolution of a Sociologist* (1971).
Richter, Melvin, *The Politics of Conscience: T. H. Green and his Age* (1964).
Schneewind, J. B., *Sidgwick's Ethics and Victorian Moral Philosophy* (1977).
Smith, K. J. M., *James Fitzjames Stephen: Portrait of a Victorian Rationalist* (1988).
Taylor, M. W., *Men versus the State: Herbert Spencer and Late Victorian Individualism* (1992).
Vincent, Andrew and Plant, Raymond, *Philosophy, Politics and Citizenship: The Life and Thought of the British Idealists* (1984).

INDEX